PAWMISTRY

PAWMISTRY

HOW TO READ YOUR CAT'S PAWS

KEN RING AND
PAUL ROMHANY

TEN SPEED PRESS
BERKELEY, CALIFORNIA

CONTENTS

intRODUCtioN

What within you wakes with day
Who can say?
All too little may we tell,
Friends who like each other well,
What might haply, if we might,
Bid us read our lives aright.
　　　　　Swinburne, from "To A Cat"

Cats have lived with us for 3,500 years, offering companionship and rodent-free housing. As the "sphinx of the hearth," however, the cat also fascinates us: an animal seemingly so close and loving, and yet in part always remaining aloof and infinitely enigmatic. Their traditional links with the gods and with the occult have certainly deepened this irresistible sense of mystery.

It is natural that we, as devoted owners, are curious about the secrets of our pets and wish to tap into their hidden depths. Moreover, we rightly feel that a more complete understanding of our loved ones will make us better and more sensitive caregivers.

This book brings to you age-old tools of divination that will let you do just that. It starts by teaching you how to interpret your cat's physiological signs—through pawmistry, skullistry, claw readings, and color—and then explores the psychic cat, the influence that numerology and the zodiac have on your cat and on you as owner.

All of the ways of reading your pet presented in *Pawmistry* are in fact ways of seeing, helping you to see what actually has been in front of you all the time. Perhaps by really looking at your cat, you too will be able to see those "different skies . . . nights with different stars" and, in so doing, be able to enjoy your cat on new and different levels.

THE PHYSICAL CAT

PAWMISTRY

THE STUDY OF THE PAW

As the hands are the servants of our human system, so too are a cat's paws symptomatic of the cat's system. In exactly the same way as with the hand and the human body, all things that affect the feline system affect the paws. Why? Because there are more nerves from the brain to the paw than to any other portion of the cat's system, so as the action of the cat's mind affects the entire body, it more immediately affects the paw. For humans this has been the rationale for palmistry; it also follows for cats.

The soft underside of our hands—our palms or paws— have been called "maps of our souls and blueprints of our lives." They reveal where we come from, where we are going, and what characteristics we have that might help or hinder our progress through life. Understanding what our palm reveals, therefore, helps clarify our sense of direction and understand and better address the stresses we are under. For the same reasons, understand ing the palms of those we love can be a very positive tool in our relationships.

The study of the paw is divided into two basic subject areas: the shape of the overall paw and the lines and markings on the large pad. Different shapes, contours, and proportions in limbs can denote culture, geographic origin, and hereditary peculiarities. Such ancestry influences temperament and aspirations and indicates what activities and lifestyles are most suitable.

What follows is an identification guide to the important indicators of your cat's paw: shape, feel, and size. However, the intermingling of breeds means that the pure or exact type is rare. More often, paws exhibit two or three types together. If you bear this in mind, you can characterize your cat and identify aspects in the cat's disposition that might otherwise be concealed or unexplained.

The two front paws reveal the most. As with humans, the left hand indicates traits you are born with, and more accurately denotes character, while the right one indicates what you become in life.

THE SHAPE OF THE PAW

Temperament is largely governed by the shape of the paw, and although a cat's paw may get broader or larger as it develops, most paws remain remarkably the same throughout life.

There are seven paw types:
- the Hunter (Earth) Paw
- the Air (Square) Paw
- the Active (Spatular) Paw
- the Knotty Paw
- the Conical Paw
- the Intuitive Paw (Water)
- the Mixed Paw

THE HUNTER/EARTH PAW

These paws are typically found on wild cats. The paw is short, large, and wide. There tend to be very few lines on the small upper pads and seldom more than the two main lines on the large pad: the Heart Line on the body side, and the Head Line. Good hunters, these cats are sure of themselves, though less trusting of humans initially. Once back in a home environment, though, they make wonderfully caring pets, perhaps as a result of their confidence. In the beginning, do not corner a Hunter because it may become disorientated and confused. This cat is courageous—"timidity" is just judicious caution. Spontaneous, they can appear to suddenly change from one personality into another.

Do not confuse the Hunter with a cat who is experiencing the "evening crazies"—the tendency for active and healthy cats to race through the house as though they were crazed (this can also erupt early in the morning)—which reflects the cat's ancient rhythm of actively hunting around dawn and dusk.

THE AIR PAW/THE USEFUL PAW

The large pad is squarish or rectangular, as wide at the bottom as it is at the top. Said to be Useful, it is found on many industrious, hardworking, and matter-of-fact cats: They do not whine for titbits but go out and hunt, returning at night to take or leave what is in the food bowl. Cats with such paws are orderly, practical, and love habit and custom, being guided by reason rather than by imagination. They respect house rules and regulations, know the basic road rules, and are noticeably methodical in their hunting and eating. They have perseverance, tenacity, and a reflective quality but can be stubborn if changes are required. Being practical, they are nearly always successful in everything they do. Although sincere, loyal, and staunch in friendship, they are not overly demonstrative, unless some reward is offered. As such, they are often described as materialistic, but this only highlights their practicality. They neither sit and wait nor sleep to excess. They can easily prowl all night and wander by day in their endless search for small material rewards.

THE ACTIVE PAW / THE IRREGULAR PAW

Also called Spatular, this paw appears crooked and irregular, being narrower at the base and wider at the top. It indicates a creative nature, restless and excitable but full of energy, of pur-

pose and enthusiasm. These are magnificent pets: They love action (be it hunting or play), are intensely energetic and independent of spirit, and love discovery. They have a strong desire to communicate and are stimulated by the new and unaccustomed, readily learning new routines. Curious to a fault, these charming cats often land themselves in hot water. If human, they would make great navigators, explorers, or discoverers.

THE KNOTTY PAW / THE SHY, PASSIVE CAT

Also referred to as the Philosophical type, the paw is usually angular and bony rather than fat and leathery. The upper pads incline inwards. These cats have a marked personality, seem indifferent to other cats and animals, including humans, and are friendly only at a distance until they get to know you. Not great hunters, they enjoy solitude and quiet and will sit for hours watching prey rather than make the effort to actually catch it. They bring to a household a notable sense of peace and harmony. Ancients believed these cats incarnated noble ancestors—they have a hint of mystery, as if they know and see far more than they would tell if they could speak.

THE CONICAL CUNNING TYPE/ THE ARISTOCRATIC CAT

A conical paw grows narrower towards the top, and the claws are particularly pointed. These cats are impulsive, quick, and clever, sometimes amazing you with their abilities. They are mentally flexible and artistically receptive. When kittens, they stand out for their alertness and the speed with which they learn. Sometimes they tire easily and are prone to overindulgence. Although this cat is forever curled up on the rug in front of the fire or heater and appears to be asleep, notice the ears swiveling. As soon as the fridge door is touched, they will spring to their feet. If they were human, these cats would become actors, dancers, or cabaret artists.

THE INTUITIVE TYPE/THE WATER PAW

Long, slender, and fragile-looking, this is the most beautiful of the paw shapes. Cats with this paw are gentle in manner and quiet in temper, and they instinctively trust everyone who is kind to them. Their intuitive faculties are highly developed, so if your cat comes and sits next to you when you are stressed, it is probably of this type. If they were human, they would be mediums or counselors because they are so alive to feelings, instincts, and impressions. Strangely, they are often the offspring of matter-of-fact, practical cats—perhaps this is the way Nature achieves balance. These cats are appreciative of everything that comes their way, and their beauty and sweet nature ensures they get along well with everyone.

THE MIXED PAW

This is the most difficult type to describe, because both the upper pads and the paw itself do not easily fit into the other categories. It is as if all the types have taken a part in the building up of this seventh type. One pad, for example, may be completely different from its adjacent one on the same paw. Versatile, these cats seem very changeable but possess multiple skills. Inside the house they are gentle and quiet, only to adopt a completely different temperament outside. They are very interesting to own and often behave like perpetual kittens (indeed, many are undersized as adults).

THE FEEL OF THE PAW

Pick up the paw and feel the texture of the pads. They should not be too thin, hard, or dry. A fleshy, soft, and somewhat clammy pad is best, indicating vitality and confidence. The pad should not be too soft and fleshy but of medium resistance to your fingers. This indicates a healthy constitution, not phlegmatic or indolent. A soft, elastic paw is a sign of energy, of enthusiasm, and of active will. A soft, flabby paw is the reverse: It denotes indolence, want of firmness of purpose, and a tendency to be more prone to the elements.

THE SIZE OF THE PAW

Generally, cats with large paws love fine movements and detail and will watch their owner for hours fascinated by whatever activity the owner is engaged in, whereas those pets with very small paws go in for big ideas and seem less interested in detail. These may hunt in impossible situations or stare for hours at a mouse hole. Even the scratchings made by small paws are often large and bold.

LEFT AND RIGHT PAWS

There is often a marked difference in the shape and position of the pads in the left and right paws of the same cat, so consider both paws. Cats have laterality, as do humans: The left paw indicates natural character; the right shows the training, experience, and surroundings brought to bear on the life of the subject. The majority of cats, like humans, are ambidextrous in most tasks.

THE PADS

Now that we have an overall feel for the paw, it is time to study in detail the components that make it up. There are two types of pads on the cat's paw: the large pad, which corresponds to the human palm, and the upper pads, which are more like the human fingers. In order to read your cat's paw, you need to be familiar with the pads and recognize the significance of what you can see.

THE LARGE PAD

The large pad expresses the strength or weakness of a cat's natural will and is one of the most significant indicators of character. It also points to health. Nerve connections between brain and limb are at their greatest where function is most concentrated. Because the large pad is instrumental in hunting, on which the cat's survival depends, the large pad is endowed with more nerves than any other area of the paw.

TWO "FEELS" OF THE LARGE PAD

Large pads come in two types: firm-jointed and supple. However, strength or weakness of will as shown by the large pad may be modified by the Heart Line, which shows the development or nondevelopment of the individual. The rule is that the shape of the paw and upper pads denotes inherited disposition, whereas the development of the lines denotes traits acquired through cultivation or environment.

The large pad, then, indicates the temperament inherited from the parent, although other characteristics might come into play.

A firm, large pad denotes obstinacy and more will and determination than present in a cat with yielding, supple pads. It is as if the firm, jointed pads are made to resist, and these cats tend to resist and fight their way more in life than cats possessing the softer pads. The character is dominant rather than exhibiting determination of purpose. A supple large pad denotes a more pliant nature, yielding readily to surrounding influences. If the Heart Line is unusually curved, however, the cat has developed will and determination that in many ways offset the inherited pliant nature.

If the claw end of the large pad is supple, the cat is more adaptable to people. If the pad is supple at the more inner region, the cat is more adaptable to circumstances. Cats with supple-jointed pads are less strict in their requirements than those possessing a firm-jointed type, and they are more adaptable.

DISTANCE OF THE LARGE PAD

The distance between the large pad and the upper pads, or claws, is also significant. The greater the distance, the more independence of will and action. Cats with a very large span will be

15

almost impossible to control or manage, will always be in trouble, and will continually ignore rules and regulations. A large pad lying close to the upper pads denotes a cat needing more love and attention and having a nervous, more timid spirit. Such cats are excessively cautious and show little interest in being independent.

DIVISIONS OF THE LARGE PAD

The large pad is divided into three mounds: the Heart Mound, the Head Mound, and the Life Mound. Each segment has a bearing on its neighbor. The Heart Mound is on the right and

is indicative of relationships and emotional well-being; the Head Mound, on the left, is about intelligence and abilities. The Life Mound is the central mound and concerns vital energy. Ideally, the Heart Mound should appear slightly larger than the Head Mound, but the Life Mound should be the largest of all three.

THE UPPER PADS

Ancient Hindi belief is that the tips of the human fingers are the habitations of the gods. Given the delicate way a cat applies its pads to a surface, one can see why cats were thought of as divine beings.

The Romans gave each pad on a cat's paw a particular name, assigning the attributes of various figures in their own mythology:

- Jupiter, the first pad (the Pad of Power): long—love of power, tyrannical; short—nonaggressive

- Saturn, the second pad (the Pad of Emotional Sensitivity): long—love of solitude; short—playfulness

- Apollo, the third pad (the Pad of Lineage or Royalty): long—snobby, proud, and confident, yet aloof; short—shy, nervy

- Mercury, the fourth pad (the Pad of Inventiveness): long—influence over and manipulation of people, deception; short—obeys commands

Further up the leg on each of the front limbs is the dewclaw. If it is long, the cat has an erratic will and is impetuous and uncertain; if it is short, the cat is surefooted and careful.

Some cats have an extra upper pad on each foot. Witches believed these cats to be endowed with more lives than the standard nine. Certainly they are more settled, with a wiser air about them.

UPPER PADS LEANING TOWARD EACH OTHER

If, after pressing lightly on the paw to open it for inspection, you let go and it falls naturally closed leaning slightly toward Jupiter (the first pad), it denotes an ambitious spirit, independence of character, and an energetic nature that is inclined to fight its way forward. If Jupiter turns towards Saturn, the reverse spirit is indicated. If Saturn turns slightly toward Apollo, expect contradictions in nature—one moment playful, the next snarling and nasty. Apollo leaning towards Mercury indicates overindulgence, probably leading to large growth.

THE SPACES BETWEEN THE UPPER PADS

A wide space between the large pad and Jupiter indicates unselfishness and independence of will. A space between Mercury and Apollo shows independence of thought, whereas a space between Saturn and Apollo shows independence of environment (will roam the neighborhood). Where there is a space between Jupiter and Saturn, independence of action is indicated.

Where the pads appear loose and are rather supple and separated, there is a dislike of restraint. If they all lie close together, the cat is more comfortable with its surroundings.

Cats whose pads are supple-jointed and curved backwards are alert and agile and can be swayed by the mood of the moment. Stiff pads curved inwards indicate less mental alertness; such cats are generally self-contained, rather quiet, and very sensitive.

LINES OF THE PAW

THE PAW CLOSE-UP

There are two important or main lines on the paw:

- the Heart Line
- the Head Line

THE HEART LINE

Two vertical lines separate the pad into three segments: the Heart Mound, the Life Mound, and the Head Mound; the Heart Line is the line on the right on the large pad.

The strength and vitality of the Heart Line indicates the strength and health of the relationships your cat has with humans and other animals. If the Heart Line goes most of the way up to the top of the pad division, these relationships will be strong all through the cat's life. If it stops halfway or less, your cat is still getting to know you and trying to work out where it fits into the household; alternatively, it needs people but also needs its own space.

Where the Heart Line crosses over onto the Life Mound, anxiety is affecting well-being. If the Life Mound is overlapping the Heart Line, the cat's sense of survival has pulled it back and made it detached from those it loves for some reason. This is probably not a permanent problem.

THE HEAD LINE

The Head Line is the line on the left of the left front paw's large pad. If the Head Line goes most of the way up, the cat is practical and gets what it wants one way or another. Such cats are resourceful and learn quickly. A Head Line that stops well short of the top does not necessarily mean less intelligence: Creativity and intuition sometimes supplement and even take over from what we think of as brightness.

If the Head Line crosses near the top, slightly onto the Life Mound, this cat may thrive and learn much because of connections formed or about to form. The present owners are perfect at the moment in this cat's life and for this pet's fulfillment. If the Life Mound leans over and slightly onto the Head Mound, the cat needs more stimulation and its needs are not yet entirely satisfied. If not doing so already, it will soon start roaming.

THE HEMISPHERES

The paw is divided into two basic hemispheres by the imaginary horizontal line that separates the upper pads from the large pad. The upper hemisphere, which comprises the pads and the fur between the pads, represents Mind and is expressed as intent and deci-sions or will. The lower hemisphere, which comprises the base of the paw, represents Body, sometimes referred to as Connectedness or Spirit.

THE HOLLOWS

At the base and at the top of the Heart and Head Lines are often seen indentations resembling upside down Vs. These Heart and Head Hollows can vary in size and depth. Most are very small if there at all, but the Heart Hollow is usually slightly larger. Hollows indicate wishes unfulfilled and dreams yet to be realized. They are more frequently seen on younger cats and diminish with age. A Heart Hollow can result if the kitten is removed too quickly from the mother, or for an adult cat if an owner is absent or unavailable for long periods. A Head Hollow can come about due to continual frustration or annoyance in hunting, or anxiety due to victimization.

THE GIRDLES

The top shapes of the three divisions of the large pad are the Head, Life, and Heart Girdles. These point to family characteristics: Gentle, unbroken curves indicate healthy genetics in each of the three areas.

Ideally, the Heart Girdle should be higher than the Head Girdle, and the Life Girdle should be even, almost horizontal and sym-metrical.

READING THE LINES

Lines should be clear, well marked, and free from breaks, islands, or irregularities. Lines that are pale or hard to define indicate lack of robust health and lack of energy or positive outcomes. Good deep-set lines denote an active, robust temperament and therefore also indicate a hopeful disposition. Remember, however, that lines may change.

THE MAIN LINES

THE HEART LINE

A perfect Heart Line—one without breaks, crosses, or crisscrossed lines of any kind, be it straight or curved across the pad—promises a healthy and long life. An exception is if the Heart Line is deep, yet what appears to be a groove travels from the top of the Heart Line across the Life Mound towards the Head Line, being the only bad mark or fantastic sign on an otherwise good paw: Indian palmists claim that a cat with this marking will be accident-prone.

THE HEAD LINE

The Head Line is to be regarded alongside and symbolic of its adjacent Mound. Sometimes a double Head Line can be faintly seen, one stronger than the other. This is a vestige of previous indecisiveness or split loyalties, now thankfully in the past. The Head Line should have a natural and relaxed look about it, neither too open nor too closed. An evenly or slightly curved line is a good sign, denoting caution; such cats are very sensitive and are generally self-confident. A balanced appearance indicates a cat with a well-balanced mental outlook.

Lines with breaks, like a chain with little hair lines, are a sign of bad health, particularly so if found on a soft paw. When the line recovers its evenness and continuity, health and vitality are regained.

The two paws must always be consulted in considering marks in illness and death; when broken on the left and joined on the right it generally means some dangerous illness impending, but if absolutely broken clean off in both pads, with lines both descending and traversing the large pad, it means premature death.

Cats with very faint Heart Lines are supersensitive, easily crushed and discouraged.

Rectify this with encouragement and training from an early age.

A faint Head Line is usually found in conjunction with a flabby, soft paw. It always denotes a restless nature craving excitement. If this faint line is sloped, the love of excitement will be gratified in gastronomic ways; in such a case the flabbiness of the paw shows an indolent nature too lazy to travel or undergo fatigue.

TRAVEL LINES

Travel lines generally involve some great change of place, climate, or country. On the upper pads, they are faint lines crisscrossing in either direction. The more widespread and deep they are, the greater the certainty that big changes are afoot.

MARKS ON THE LINES

A mark on the Heart Line denotes illness or loss of health for as long as the mark lasts, but a large, clear mark at the very left of the line indicates some mystery surrounding the cat's birth.

Marks on or near the Head Line denote robust health and a fighting disposition and are an excellent sign on a cat living close to water as it shows courage and love of danger.

21

Sometimes spots appear on the upper pads. When they appear on Jupiter and Saturn, they may signal an aggressive nature, aroused by the slightest opposition.

The Lesser Lines
Base Line of the Heart Mound

The Base Lines form the bottom edges of the three mounds of the large pad. The Base Line of the Heart Mound defines the strength of territoriality. If clear and unbroken, the cat has powerful scent and visual signaling systems, well-developed homing skills, and the tendency to fiercely protect the boundaries of its environment. Very often these cats become involved in noisy disputes; in most cases this is temporary. Those with less distinct lines tend to have smaller territories, requiring only enough area for their daily needs. Horizontal lines branching off the Base Lines in a female indicate how many litters she will have or has the potential to have; in a male it indicates the number of times he will mate.

Base Line of the Head Mound

This is the line of communication. Cats with this line deeply visible are great communicators, not just with the person who feeds and shelters them, but with other (usually carefully selected) humans, other cats, and even other animals. Such cats are very vocal.

Base Line of the Life Mound

A line of protection, it touches on all worldly affairs; success and failure, barriers and obstacles, and the influence of people and other cats. If absent or faint, the cat is more susceptible to bad influences and diseases. A clearly defined line protects the cat's own efforts, keeps the personality strong, and indicates success.

Sample Quick Reading

Look at the cat's left front paw and note the shape of the Girdles. Looking at the Life Girdle, focus on whether or not it dips down in the center like a V. If it does, the cat lacks energy when it comes to tasks like catching insects. This may be simply that it does not waste energy on fruitless missions or it looks before it leaps and it spends a lot of time in meditation. These cats value rests and are too intelligent to race around aimlessly. Extremely well mannered and sensitive, they make very good housecats who learn things quickly. If the Life Girdle is like an upside down V, the cat has a remarkable energy level. It never sits still but is always chasing something—insects, mice, birds; there is never a dull moment, and something is always going on that will interest it. If the Life Girdle is straight or horizontal, the cat is very level headed. Its motto is "Steady as you go," and it does not like change.

Look at the general shape of the paw. If it is parallel all the way up at the sides, the cat is loyal and confident and will fight for its territory if it feels any threat because its sense of belonging is very strong. It does not roam but prefers to stick to a fairly small locality. If the paw widens at the top, the cat loves exploring —its curiosity is boundless. This makes such cats excellent mouse-catchers. If the paw is narrower at the top, they appreciate fine things and delicacy. This is not to say they are not good hunters, but they have a sense of extreme gentleness, which is unusual in such an active animal!

Notice what the cat is doing during the reading. If it sits quietly, it is very much a people's cat and cannot get enough smooching and petting. It is healthy and will live a long life, and its harmony is also likely to help its owner to have a long life.

Finally, feel the firmness of the pads and any resistance to their being gently pressed. Glance into the cat's eyes: If this pressing is at all unpleasant, the cat will flinch and try to take its paw away. If it does, it may be unhappy at being in a strange place or with a stranger, or it may be coming down with something, so keep an eye on your cat for the next few days. If it is happy with the action, it is healthy and confident and feels fulfilled.

THE CLAWS

Normally there are four claws per paw. Rear claws do not grow as quickly and are not as sharp. Claws are one of the most interesting sections of the study of the cat's paw because they not only indicate temperament but are also remarkably sure guides to hereditary tendencies towards disease.

To examine your cat's claws, set your cat down securely in the crook of your arm, with the cat either in your lap or on the floor between your knees. Pin the cat to your side and hold one of its paws with your hand. With its back away from you, it cannot scratch you or easily get away. If you squeeze your cat's paw with your free hand, the claws will come out. Examine them carefully. If you have trouble holding the cat still, get someone to help—but be careful because this often means you will then be in front of its claws and vulnerable. If this procedure is too difficult, analyze your cat's constitution from the slices of claws it sheds.

If the claws are white, the difference between the nail and the quick is easy to see in good lighting. The quick is the pink tissue visible within the nail of the claw at the base.

Different claws grow at different rates; check them periodically because this will indicate much about a cat's disposition. Checking regularly not only tells you much about your cat's well-being, but also reduces the cat's anxiety about being in that position.

Types of Claws

Cats can have four types of claws:

● long claws—not associated with physical strength; easier to train and gentle natured

● short claws—cats have more energy and are generally fidgety and flighty, so they need space to move and places to explore

● broad claws—an independent and proud nature, where claws are broader than they are long; these cats can appear obstinate and hard to coerce

● narrow claws—cooperative, easy to get along with, these cats have a peaceful and loving nature; thin, very small claws can denote delicate health and lack of vitality

Health Indications

● Long, narrow claws are signs of weakness of the back and, if extremely narrow and much curved, later spinal trouble (long claws that are wide at the top can be a sign of previous illness and full recovery).

● Claws without quick denote some energy decrease (can be hereditary), with a tendency for bad circulation and weak action of the heart.

● Short claws, flat and sunken into the flesh, are a warning for limb paralysis later in life.

● Short claws, flat and inclined to lift or curl out at the edges, signal impending nervous disorder, particularly if the base of the claw is bluish.

● Short-clawed cats suffer more heart troubles and maladies affecting the trunk and back in later life; long-clawed cats suffer in the lungs, chest, throat, and head. When claws are curved the tendency is accentuated.

● Fluted claws indicate a delicate constitution; when, however, the fluted claws are broken by corrugations across the claw, growth in the claw is arrested, suggesting delicacy.

● Ribbed claws indicate delicacy of the constitution and an inherited propensity towards colds, so no matter how strong the cat appears to be, make sure it can keep warm. Long line of domestication is also indicated.

● Large quick indicates increased forces of circulation and rapid action of the heart; this cat will not want to sit around all day resting.

● White spots all over the claws are a sign of tension, possibly indicating recent nervous strain or fear.

Note: When sick, cats become inactive to conserve energy. A sick cat may seem lifeless but will recover after a few days of withdrawal, which is why cats have been said to have nine lives. Nonetheless, always take a sick cat to a veterinarian.

THE PAWS OF KITTENS

Initially kittens live completely in their inner reality, interpreting everything that happens to them through their imaginary world. Gradually they awaken and must adapt to external reality, part of which is accepting and recognizing what offers them security. The way in which they do this is critical to their future development. Parallel to this are the mother's efforts to slowly distance herself from her offspring, so that the young kitten will learn to be independent. This process, too, greatly affects kittens' attitudes to their world.

Similarly, the way you treat your kitten is fundamental to its development. The key rule is: Let the kitten develop at its own pace. Belated development can be caused by the kitten's natural disposition, and this is revealed in its paw. Trying to raise a kitten against its natural disposition can cause irreparable damage in later life, whether physical or spiritual. Kittens whose development is belated and slow are able to preserve their vital energies and achieve greater and more valuable results later in life than kittens whose development is too rapid and thus come to an earlier standstill. Precocious kittens may make amazing progress up to the second or third year, but their paws will show that this premature development has exacted an unwarranted expenditure of energy, thus endangering their nervous strength and their inner life. The sign of precociousness is the Base Line of the Life Mound, the line of energy, running along the base of the large pad. If it appears forked in any part of its length, training and reward systems for this kitten should be carefully supervised.

Pawmistry can do three things, then: indicate the kitten's natural disposition; reveal why development is being impeded or what damage has been caused by inappropriate development; guide you towards compensating for any damage. This involves not just disposition but also the influence of ancestors. From the first month, the paw of a kitten clearly shows its dispositions with all their subsidiary traits, particularly in the right (ancestral) paw. The left paw expresses individual personality.

Divisions of the Paw
The Outer Paw

Tempting though it is to concentrate on a striking or unusual feature and make it the pivot of the final evaluation of the kitten's personality, always interpret features in the light of all the other factors supplied by the outer paw—the pads, the claws, the distances between pads, the Line shapes, and so forth.

First, ascertain the expressional tendency of the kitten paw. What does the outside of the paw (the area above and on top of the large pad) reveal? This general expression—i.e., lively and animated versus rigid and inexpressive—conveys the spiritual quality, the inner standard, and the seed and nucleus of the personality.

While the outer paw reveals the static element of the personality, the inner paw reveals its dynamics. The static element is the inherited disposition, the biological husk, as it were, which so far has not revealed to what extent the dispositions have been active. For example, the shape and appearance of the claws may reveal a disposition to lung diseases, yet the kitten need never be affected by it. Investigation might show, however, a family history of the ailment.

The Inner Paw

The dynamic element, revealed by the inner paw, is the effect that the environment and the experiences have upon disposition and inherited traits. As with the pads, a striking difference in the expression and form of the right and left paws is of special significance. If both outer paws are essentially different, we can assume that the character or temperament of the

parent cats must have differed greatly from each other. This divergency can affect the personality either as conflicting forces that impede development, or as positive and productive forces when united and operating together.

PAW SHAPES

There are three main kitten paw shapes, and one additional but much rarer type, although the three fundamental types hardly ever occur in their pure form. The names and shapes of these types are the same as for adult cats (see earlier section). To ascertain the shape of the paw, study the back of the paw and the pads separately, for individual pads may differ in form from the others as well as from the back of the paw. The three common types are

- the Air Paw
- the Conical Paw
- the Spatular Paw

The less common type is
- the Hunter

The back of the kitten's paw tells you something about its practical intelligence. Look at the relative size of the back of the paw and the pad areas. If equal, a certain harmony and balance is indicated. If the back of the paw is larger and wider than the upper pad area, however, the practicalities of life will outweigh development in a higher sense, both emotionally and spiritually—this kitten above all else is a survivor. If the upper pad area predominates, then the practical abilities are neglected and this cat might rather sit around and wait for things to happen, preferring to live in a world of feline imagination.

PAW VERUS BODY

The size of the paw and the size of the kitten's body should be well proportioned. Too big a body for too small a paw may lead to a lack of restraining power of the personality, leading to lack of self-control, restlessness, and difficulty concentrating. Small kittens with paws too large will be more emotional, fearful, and enthusiastic, more inclined to act and react impulsively. Their feet are nimble and quick, so they are excellent climbers.

THE CLAWS

The claws of a kitten are especially relevant for the detection of disease.

COLOR

The normal color should be pinky white. If pale white, the kitten may be anemic. Paleness in one claw indicates just one organ is affected. The first claw (corresponding to a human index finger) could be stomach, liver, gall, or spleen; the second claw (corresponding to the human ring finger) could mean nervous or cardiac disorders; the third claw (our middle finger) could mean intestines; and the fourth claw (our little finger) might correspond to testicles, bladder, ovaries, uterus, and kidneys.

Red claws indicate that the composition of blood is lacking in phosphorus, calcium, or iron, or that the distribution of red and white corpuscles is bad. Blood pressure may be too high.

Bluish claws point to vascular trouble, circulatory disturbances, and a possible weak heart.

SPOTS

When white dots appear on the claws, it helps to know if they have always been there or just appeared. If the latter, it denotes lack of sleep or fatigue. Permanent dots are a sign of alimentary complaints or, later, rheumatism.

RIBBING

If the claws are ribbed lengthwise as well as breadthwise, as well as being pale, we can guess almost with certainty that an illness is in the process of starting.

SCRATCHINGS

HANDWRITING ANALYSIS

Writing is a means of communication, and cats leave their mark just as humans do. Cats express themselves in much the same way as small children, and similarly enjoy expressing themselves in artistic ways without thought to cost of materials or damage (be it carpet, furniture, or walls). In this chapter, we interpret exactly what your cat is telling you in its "etchings."

Size

Smaller scratchings indicate a desire to concentrate realistically on a small field of focus. These cats may be fearful, shy, or trying to work out a problem, like a new environment, and they need reassurance. Large lines reveal a desire to expand or extend fields of interest. This may mean they are about to wander or, alternatively, they may be pleased with themselves after a recent hunting venture.

Slant

Like humans, cats show a left- or right-pawed writing preference. Most are right-pawed, possibly because humans subconsciously pass some species preference on to cats, by stroking them with the right hand, serving food on the right, placing bowls on the right, etc.

Left Slant

A left-paw will write with a left slant. This is sometimes interpreted as defiance and resistance to environment. Mostly it indicates a contemplative and passive nature, a cat liable to stay inside its "shell" and hide its emotions. The cat has not cut off completely from the past—its origins, unpleasant memories, and early experiences. The left is the sign of femininity and may also be a plus in terms of gentleness.

Upright

Upright scratchings indicate self-reliance,

poise, calm, reserve, a neutral attitude, and self-sufficiency.

RIGHT SLANT

This shows an involvement with the environment, leaning forward toward others, the future, and the common goal of the house. These cats want to communicate and are emotionally responsive and demonstrative. They tend to worry and depend on others.

CHANGES IN SLANT

Scratchings both to left and right in the same piece indicate a cat with changing inclinations and views, one who is presently on a learning curve. As such, the cat may be unpredictable to itself and others, "trying to find itself." This can arise from having parents of different temperaments, genetically pulling the kitten in different directions.

WIDTH

NARROW

Cats, like humans, can be narrow-minded. A narrow-line-scratcher may be well disciplined and well trained, but it may feel restricted and confined. Inner inhibitions and fears may cramp its personality. Alternatively, it might just want to escape from a small room to the great outdoors once in a while.

BROAD

The broad scratcher has an inner desire for expansion. These cats are uninhibited and like to have elbow room and spread themselves about. They will not have just one resting place but several, over a wide area.

ZONES

A scratcher confronted with a broad surface is symbolically confronted with its own position in space and time, its attitude to itself and others, to the past and future. To the left is kittenhood and the past; to the right are the future, work to be done, and fellow creatures. Any surface is a zone, with upper, middle, and lower divisions.

LARGE UPPER ZONE WITH SMALL MIDDLE AND LOWER ZONES

This cat's needs are presently not being met. Perhaps it wants to sleep on the bed but is not allowed and can only tell you so by "writing it all down" in this way. These cats feel no roots or foundations to their personality. Although they achieve a great deal because they are motivated to strive, they lack balance and consideration, and their endeavors may not be substantiated in reality. Their head is in the air. They are calling out for reassurance.

SMALL UPPER AND LOWER ZONES WITH LARGE MIDDLE ZONE

Striving and aspirations are supported by physical stamina and a materialistic outlook, but these cats lack inner calm. They are dissatisfied by what comes their way, always looking for more of everything!

SMALL UPPER ZONE, AVERAGE MIDDLE ZONE, AND LARGE LOWER ZONE

This shows strong material and instinctive drive, very down-to-earth and earthy. This cat likes life's pleasures and has little other motivation than the pursuit of pleasure.

LARGE MIDDLE AND LOWER ZONES WITH SMALL UPPER ZONE

This shows a strong social self-confidence, social involvement, strong material and instinctive drive, and little aspiration upwards. They are contented and happy in their role and know their place in the house.

LARGE UPPER AND MIDDLE ZONES WITH SMALL LOWER ZONE

This is a cat with high ambitions and good self-confidence, but a personality with no deep roots. Instinct is repressed because it is fearful of doing the wrong thing. It could have an explosive personality, suddenly reacting in a snarl or a flinch.

LARGE MIDDLE ZONE WITH SMALL UPPER AND LOWER ZONES

These cats live in the here and now; grandeur and involvement are their way of life. They do not have high aspirations and do not want to rush outside at every opportunity, nor are they motivated much toward hunting endlessly. They sometimes get bored and feel confined.

REGULARITY

Some scratchings have even-sized lines, and others vary. Regularity denotes a steady cat, disciplined, regular as clockwork. Such cats have a sense of duty, are predictable, and can be relied on to behave in an orderly manner. But they can be rather dull and lack playfulness. Where scratchings are irregular, the cats can be disorderly, knocking things over on shelves. They lack steadiness, but crave variety and change. Often they feel imprisoned and trapped, emotional, frustrated, never dull or predictable, hectic, unsettled, and all over the place. Alternatively, they may be undergoing some personal change or changing their priorities.

CONNECTION AND DISCONNECTION

Where the scratchings are disconnected, the cats are attracted to whims and detail, not to the whole. They find it difficult to make friends because they cannot see the payoff. They will run up a tree after a bird without first figuring if there is an easy way down. But they are not morose complainers. Connected scratchings reveal that thoughts are linked with one another, and they can see and understand relationships. Their personality has strength and integration.

PRESSURE

Overall heavy pressure can mean strong reserves of energy, vitality, and vigor, or indicate a cat who can be feeling things deeply. It could be a case of a "heavy hand and a heavy heart": Such cats may need time spent with them to overcome a notion of being neglected.

SPACING

Wide spacing between scratch lines is the work of cats who want to keep their distance. They are stand-offish and picky in their choice of friends. They do not like people breathing down their neck and may feel hemmed in by children of the house. Wide spaces are an attempt at self-imposed loneliness and isolation. Narrow spacing shows an inability to keep distance and a lack of respect for boundaries and restrictions.

MARGINS

Cats who scratch right up to the edge of their surface and leave no margin cling to the past, are insecure, and need love, security, and contact. They have their own areas, which, if disturbed, make them rather tense. Narrow margins indicate a desire to stay on top and denote a lack of respect of others.

S K U L L i S T R Y

BVMPS OꞀ THE HEAD AꞀD THEiR MEAꞀiꞀG

The head is the body's most sensitive organ. "Skullistry" divides the cat's head into 30 areas or organs (humans have 42). Studying the size, shape, and bumps on your cat's head can help you work out what kind of loving animal your cat is.

PROCESS

There may be one bump on each side of the skull—the Love Bump—which indicates the power to love and be loved. If you can feel this on your cat's head, below the ears and directly on the back of the head roughly level with the eyes, you have a very loving cat, one that regards you as its entire world, as its surrogate parent and closest companion. If your cat has two or more, you don't know how lucky you are. But those bumps may be elsewhere, according to the illustration. Sometimes fatty deposits under the skin give a false reading. Move the bump under your fingers and see if it shifts with the skin.

IꞀTERPRETATIOꞀ

Following is a quick guide to what the bumps mean, according to the skull-position number.

1—This shows just how interested your cat is in you. Bumps in similar places on both sides of the skull show it probably dreams about you!

2—This indicates a faithful and loyal cat who is contentedly living in your house.

3 (bump slightly higher)—A gentle family cat who knows what it wants and who it needs to protect but cannot work out who actually belongs in the house.

4 (bump down the side slightly, although farther up the neck)—Generous and patient, this cat is aware you are busy and will accommodate your lifestyle even if it does not always approve.

5 (in the middle)—Bumps here indicate jealousy: You have been spending more time with another.

6—Your cat misses you and worries when you leave the house.

7—A contented cat with no hang-ups.

8—This bump is for memory. The cat worries about what it thinks will happen based on what it knows about you.

9—This cat wants more than it is getting (in its opinion). Sometimes it gets fed up and has to leave the house.

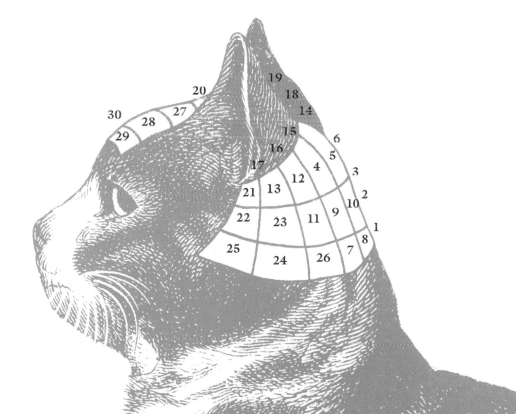

10—A proud cat who gets annoyed quickly when its physical contact desires are unfulfilled.

11—This cat worries about your business deals and finances and thinks you are taking too many risks. It wants to comfort you.

12—This cat would rather be loved than fed. A very sensitive cat with deep feelings.

13—When it purrs it is singing a love song to you!

14—This cat feels let down and jilted. A pat, scratch, and tickle will fix everything.

15 (almost on the ear)—The cat values warmth and friends and will allow anyone to like it but will only really share its heart with you.

16—This cat is very sensitive to sounds and smells. It knows when something is wrong by your smell: It needs reassurance that you are okay.

17 (at the corner of the ear)—You are right for each other. This cat feels it is here for a healing mission and will serve you until the end.

18—It misses curling up in your lap like it used to.

19 (in the middle behind the ears)—This cat knows you inside and out—and does not always approve of your choice of friends.

20 (right between the ears)—Slightly confused as to your feelings. You seem to come and go with your affections.

21 (base of the ears)—This cat feels like a kitten again when you stroke it. It places its soul in your hands and asks that you be gentle with it.

22—Your cat knows you are busy but needs you to give it a very quick peck anyway.

23—A bump here means a mature cat who knows it has much to be thankful for.

24—This cat has not yet worked out your routines because they seem to change. It is not happy but keeps a brave face and loves you anyway.

25 (side of the head, level with the eyes)—This cat understands your workload and does not give up on you.

26—This cat compares itself to others and feels unappreciated. However, food will more than make up for lack of demonstrative affection.

27—If this cat were human it would be waiting for you to return, holding a rolling pin! Where were you? Who were you with?

28—This cat frets easily: It has been crying internally over a recent upset.

29—This cat wants to go everywhere with you and looks for you when you are gone.

30—(in the middle above the eyes)—You drive them wild with annoyance or ecstasy!

CAT COLORS

COLORS AND THEIR MEANING

At birth, kittens lack distinctive coloring, and many do not acquire their characteristic markings and color for weeks. Nonetheless, colors and personalities work together. In this chapter, we look at the broad range of colors and patterns, although many variations are genetically possible. Note, the term "red" is used to describe the color that is commonly called "orange," "marmalade," or "ginger." "Blue" is the color commonly called "gray" or "maltese."

TABBIES

One of the most common colors, the tabby pattern dates back to domestic cats in ancient Egypt. Thought to be the "wild" type, it is a recognized color variety in purebred cats and is frequently seen in cats of mixed ancestry. Tabby coloring is highly variable, but for show cats it should consist of the following dark markings: stripes and whorls on the face and cheeks; a pattern like butterfly wings across the shoulders; two rings around the chest; bands on the back and sides; and rings around the legs and tail. Tabby colors are generally brown, silver gray, bluish ivory, and reddish brown.

All tabbies have thin pencil lines on the face, expressive markings around the eyes, and an M between their eyebrows. If you look closely at the light parts of a tabby's coat, you will see that the individual hairs are striped with alternating light and dark bands, like the fur of a rabbit or a squirrel. This banding is called "agouti."

PATTERNS

There are four different tabby patterns:

• *mackerel tabby*—the "tiger," cats have narrow stripes that run in parallel down their sides; often described as having a mind of their own

• *classic ("blotched") tabby*—they have bold, swirling patterns on their sides like marble cake; some call them more of an inside cat because they like being pampered

• *spotted tabby*—they have spots all over their sides (sometimes large, sometimes small, sometimes they appear to be broken mackerel stripes) and have acquired a reputation for fearlessness

• *ticked tabby*—sometimes called the "Abyssinian tabby" or "agouti tabby," they do not have stripes or spots on their body but have tabby markings on the face and agouti hairs on the body (the Abyssinian color also appears in nonpurebreds, but it does not mean they are Abyssinian)

COLORS

Tabbies come in many different colors. You can tell what color a tabby is by looking at the color of its stripes and its tail tip. The color of the agouti hairs (the "ground color") may vary tremendously, from washed-out to rich tones. Colors include

• *brown tabby*—they have black stripes on a brownish or grayish ground color (the "black" stripes may be coal-black or a little bit brownish) and are very territorial

• *blue tabby*—they have gray stripes on a grayish or buff ground color (the stripes may be a dark slate gray or a lighter blue-gray) and are valued for their hunting prowess

• *red tabby*—they have orange stripes on a cream ground color (the stripes may be dark reddish orange or light "marmalade" orange) and dote on affection and warmth, making good pets for older people

• *cream tabby*—they have cream stripes on a pale cream ground color (the stripes look sand-colored or peach-colored rather than orange) and are calm and friendly, frequently liking endless grooming

• *silver tabby*—they have black stripes on a white ground color, the roots of the hairs being white (there are also blue silver and cream silver tabbies and the red silver "cameo" tabby, depending on the color of the stripes); in all cases, silver tabbies have a pale ground color and white roots; these beautiful creatures will end up running your household for you

SOLIDS AND SMOKES

SOLIDS

If your cat is pretty much the same color all over, it is a "solid." In personality terms, solids are just like their colors: always there and always reliable. Examples include

- *solid black*—black all over (whether coal black, grayish black, or brownish black), they can "rust" in the sunlight, their coat turning a lighter brownish shade; historically they have been associated with witchcraft and the occult and suggest mysteriousness, secrecy, and the cover of night
- *solid blue*—also called "maltese," they are blue-gray all over (whether dark slate gray, a medium gray, or a pale ash gray); this is the color of the Russian Blue, Chartreux, and Korat, but it can appear in almost any other breed as well and also in nonpurebreds
- *solid white*—white all over, their eyes may be blue, green, or gold (or have one blue eye and one green eye, the "odd-eyed white"); they are pleasant to be around and ideal as a first kitten

Most solid-colored cats are the result of a recessive gene that suppresses the tabby pattern. However, if the tabby pattern is not totally suppressed, you might see indistinct "shadow" tabby markings in certain lights, even on a solid black cat. The tabby-suppressing gene is not effective on red or cream cats, who always have tabby markings. Solid white cats are the result of a gene that suppresses color completely. Young white cats often have vague smudges of color on the top of the head where the color is not completely suppressed, and sometimes this persists.

SMOKES

If your cat is solid black or gray but the roots of the hairs are distinctly white, it is a "smoke." Whereas it is normal for the roots on a solid cat to be grayish, true smokes have definite white roots. Smokes are the solid version of silver tabbies. These cats are meticulously clean and meow only tentatively after much hesitation. They are docile and even-tempered. Smokes include

- *black smoke*—solid black with white roots
- *blue smoke*—solid blue (gray) with white roots

CATS WITH WHITE MARKINGS

Clearly delineated white markings (as opposed to shaded points, like the Siamese) can appear on any color. Just add "and white" to the cat's

- *harlequin*—mostly white with several large patches of color
- *van*—almost all white with color patches only on the head and tail

There are a couple of affectionate, informal terms used for black and white cats:
- *tuxedo cat*—a black and white cat with white paws, chest, and belly, possibly with some white on the face as well
- *jellicle cat*—after T. S. Eliot's poem in *Old Possum's Book of Practical Cats*

Torties, Patched Tabbies, and Calicos

If your cat is randomly patched with different colors, you probably have a tortie, patched tabby, or calico. These cats have a mixed heredity and, because of years of deliberate cross-breeding, are totally domesticated.

Names for cats without white markings
- *tortoiseshell,* or *tortie*—randomly patched all over with red, black, and cream (the patches may be very mingled or they may be more distinct)
- *blue-cream* (also called *blue tortie* or *dilute tortie*)—randomly patched all over with a soft, pastel blue and cream

basic color to describe the cat. So, for example, your cat might be a "black and white" or a "cream tabby and white."

There are different names for the different amounts of white:
- *mitted*—white paws only
- *locket*—white spot on the chest (in ancient times a cat with a locket was said to be the holder of secrets)
- *buttons*—one or more little white belly spots
- *bicolor*—about half white, this cat is lusty and adventurous, often highly strung and intensely emotional, the two colors indicating two basic genetic lineages and therefore combining two distinct personalities in a new form

• *brown-patched tabby*—looks almost like autumn leaves, with patches of brown tabby and patches of red tabby (also known as *torbie* because it is a tabby tortie)

• *blue-patched tabby*—a soft color, with patches of blue tabby and patches of cream tabby

• *Russian Blue*—noted for the quality of their short, plushlike coat, they are characteristically quiet and gentle, are solidly colored blue-gray, and have round, green eyes and soft, silky fur that resembles sealskin in texture; fine-boned cats with long, slim legs and slender bodies, they have relatively long, tapering tails and wedge-shaped heads; the ears are large, broad at the base and pointed at the tips

Cats with a lot of white are inclined to be more home-based, whereas those with darker colors make better hunters and outdoor cats. There is special terminology for tortoiseshells with white markings, depending on how much white they have:

• *tortoiseshell and white* or *blue-cream and white*—only small white areas, the body has mingled colors

• *calico*—more white (as a rule, the more white there is, the larger and more distinct the red and black patches will be; large black patches are solid black, whereas large red patches are actually red tabby)

• *dilute calico*—the same amount of white as a calico, but instead of red and black patches, they have blue and cream patches (the blue patches are solid blue, and the cream patches are cream tabby)

• *patched tabby and white* or *torbie and white*—may have any amount of white (a patched tabby with a lot of white, like a calico, has large distinct patches of color and is sometimes called a *patterned calico,* a *calico tabby,* or *calihy)*

POINTED (SIAMESE) CATS

If your cat has dark "points" (face, paws, and tail) shading to a much lighter color on the body, it is a "pointed" cat. This is the pattern of the Siamese cat, but many other breeds as well as nonpurebreds also come in this pattern. This pattern is sometimes called the "color point" or "himalayan" pattern (not to be confused with the purebreds with similar names). Pointed cats are born white and gradually darken with age.

Pointed cats come in many different colors:

• *seal point*—dark brown points and a body color anywhere between light brown and ivory

- *blue point*—gray points and a light gray or beige body
- *lynx point*—tabby points in any of the colors described in the tabby section, e.g., a "blue lynx point" or "red lynx point"; the body color may show some shadow tabby markings, especially as the cat gets older
- *tortie point*—tortoiseshell points

Blue-cream points and *patched tabby* points are also possible. You can even have a pointed cat with white markings! If the cat has a lot of white, however, it can be hard to see the pointed pattern (especially on the feet). White markings will cover up any other color where they appear.

Longhair

Noted for its long, soft, flowing coat, long-haired cats were originally known as Persians or Angoras. The longhair—a medium-sized or large cat with a cobby (stocky), short-legged body—has a broad, round head, a snub nose, and a short, heavily haired tail. The large, round eyes may be blue, orange, golden, green, or copper-colored, depending on the color of the cat. The soft, finely textured coat forms a heavy ruff about the neck.

The longhair is bred in a number of color varieties. The solid, or self, colors are white, black, blue, red, and cream. Patterned coats include shaded silver and black (smoke); silver, brown, blue, or red with darker markings

(tabby); white finely ticked with black (chinchilla); cream, red, and black (tortoiseshell); calico or tortoiseshell and white; blue-gray and cream intermingled (blue cream); and bicolored. The colors of tortoiseshells, calicos, and blue creams are genetically linked with the sex of the cat: Almost all are females, and most of the few males are sterile. Blue-eyed white cats have a tendency to be deaf.

Longhairs with Siamese markings (i.e., pale body and dark face, ears, legs, and tail) are himalayans or color-points. Similarly marked longhairs with white paws are called Birmans. Peke-faced longhairs have short, pushed-in, Pekingese-like faces.

Longhair cats, although generally considered more languorous than shorthaired cats, are noted for playfulness, affection, and the ability to defend themselves if necessary.

FREQUENTLY ASKED QUESTIONS

ARE TORTOISESHELL CATS ALWAYS FEMALE?

Tortoiseshell and related colors (blue cream, patched tabby, calico, etc.) are the result of a sex-linked gene and require two X chromo-somes to appear. Generally speaking, these colors will only appear in females. Very rarely, these colors may appear in male cats, but these males are genetically abnormal (they have XXY instead of the normal XY) and are almost always infertile.

WHAT EYE COLORS ARE POSSIBLE?

Eye color is genetically related to coat color. Pointed cats always have blue eyes. White cats, and cats with a lot of white markings, can have blue, green, gold, or copper eyes or "odd eyes" (one blue eye and one green or gold eye). Other cats can have only green, gold, or copper eyes, not blue eyes. The most common eye colors are in the middle of the eye color spectrum (greenish-yellow to gold). The colors at the ends of the eye color spectrum (deep green or brilliant copper) are usually seen only in purebreds who have been selectively bred for extreme eye color, but they may sometimes appear in nonpurebreds.

ARE WHITE CATS ALWAYS DEAF?

No. If they have blue eyes, they are more likely to be deaf than a white cat with gold or green eyes.

THE PSYCHIC CAT

ΠUMEROLOGY

ΠUMBERS AND THEIR MEANING

The age-old study of numbers gives you a knowledge of the cosmic forces governing your cat's life. Just by doing simple arithmetic around your name and your cat's name, you can fine tune your intuition and, by so doing, explain some of the past, solve problems in the present, and predict the future. This will give you an inside understanding of your cat and make you a more empathetic companion.

Use numerology in conjunction with pawmistry to check one system against the other for accuracy.

PROCESS

First spell out your name. This can be your first name, last name, or nickname; it should be the name you are comfortably known by. Then spell out the name of your cat. Add the letter values of each name, using this formula:

a	b	c	d	e	f	g	h	i
1	2	3	4	5	6	7	8	9

j	k	l	m	n	o	p	q	r
1	2	3	4	5	6	7	8	9

s	t	u	v	w	x	y	z
1	2	3	4	5	6	7	8

Add totals to get the final number, until you have a final single-digit number.

Example: a cat named Mishka

M	4
I	9
S	1
H	8
K	2
A	1
Total	25
	2 + 5 = 7

So 7 is Mishka's number. Read the following section on "interpretation," to find out the character of a cat with number 7.

Naming Your Cat

T. S. Eliot wrote, "The Naming of Cats is a difficult matter, / It isn't just one of your holiday games." Penguin Books publishes a list of common and popular cat names for those who are wondering what to call their cat and need inspiration. Use numerology to find out the significance of your choice.

Interpretation

1 or 10: Top Cat, they stand alone, know what they want and where and how to get it. Unhappy when other animals are around, they resent strangers and visitors unless they are giving goodies. These cats are here to win, take one day at a time, and do not hold grudges. They live fearlessly and are masters at anticipating your next move! They will always be young at heart and will bring youth and joy to you, too. They have their own idea of how things should be done and may reverse the recognized order of the day just to be different. Independent, yet sensitive, they guard their plans carefully.

2: The Manipulator of their owner, they make their feelings known in no uncertain terms if anything is bothering them. They whine for attention, nag, and like nothing better than to be fondled. Refusing to take life seriously, they are wise and alert, living on their wits. They love companionship and music and, it is said, possess powers of the occult. One never knows who will be the uppermost: you or them. They want cooperation through peace and harmony, are unassuming, but have a hypnotic power that can bring you around to their way of thinking. They always weigh one thing against another and sometimes cannot decide what to do. Born for adventure— and the limelight!

3: Joyousness, this number represents the Eternal Child. The whole world revolves around them, they think—and rightly so! 3 is a blend of 1 and 2, and adds to a home the concept of a family trinity. Sometimes a 3 never grows up. They are very vocal and have the ability to cement a family and bring peace to conflict. They are friendly, sympathetic, and splendid judges of foods. Inclined to be a little emotional, they nevertheless teach you about true unconditional love. Good-natured, they have a talent for making friends.

4: The number for Work, of executing Plans. They know they must hunt and earn their keep and are quite comfortable fulfilling a useful role for the benefit of others. They are unusually concerned with cleanliness and order and routines. They know what they can do and won't waste time on a useless mission that has no payoff. They are keen and like to keep busy, and consequently they will live to a ripe age. They cannot quite approve of people sitting around and resting. The number for Loyalty, this cat will not forget you in its thoughts and plans. Even though they appear to be industrious and pass you by, your welfare is their prime concern. They are inspired hustlers and do not get too concerned with pleasures for themselves.

5: Being 4 + 1, these self-directed cats say little but get a lot done in a day. They will not moan for assistance or constant handouts but will go off and do much themselves to earn their food. They will make a dash for independence quietly if they can see the opportunity, before others are aware that they have gone. Adaptable, loving change and new experiences, there is never a dull moment with these cats! They are free as the air, brisk and bustling, with a nose for new things. This is the kitten who gets stuck up trees and on poles and cannot get down. Their adventures may appear foolhardy, but in their eyes they are real explorers. They have magnetic personalities and love walking.

6: 2 x 3, also 1 + 2 + 3. They have all the attributes of these numbers and more. A 6 makes for a strong combination of (1) analysis and gathering together of people, (2) making something happen, and (3) reality. There is a strong pull toward home, mating, and offspring. They like to feel responsible, as if they own the place

but look after it too. They can make themselves at home no matter where they are.

7: 4 + 3. They desire the best or none at all. They are like a stately pine tree, more dignified than the rest. They have come to occupy the stage, and their word is final in their world. They are sensitive to atmosphere and personalities and may hide real feelings by apparent indifference. They dislike mingling with the common crowd. They do not move easily, unless they have to, and then with a quick and final agility. They are not always understood, but their heart is pure gold. These cats value appreciation like no other. You have a treasure here.

8: 2 x 4. A cat with this number has twice the potential for hunt-oriented success and personal feelings of health and satisfaction. They will very quickly set in motion their own rhythm of regularity. They are born managers, able to keep several people busy and happy at the same time. When you are on time with their food they are hugely impressed and appreciative. These cats do not forget favors. They can transform enemies into friends, ideas into plans, and plans into tangible results. They know how to turn on the power and keep things moving.

9: This number includes all the other numbers. It is also 3 x 3. These cats are like a radiant sun whose warming rays have the power to make those around them grow and bloom. Their magnetism, reaching farther, brings a greater reaction too than of a less vital cat. So be careful not to upset them: They feel criticism very deeply because they love very deeply. They enjoy long trips. These cats will share their food bowl with anyone.

11: Born for the limelight and adventure, these cats are sensitive and psychic. Sometimes they get fidgety and cannot stay in one place. If they can bridle their impulsiveness, they have the makings of a master. Fond of music.

COMPATIBILITIES BETWEEN OWNER AND CAT

5 and 1: These two have much in common. Both love change, variety, and freedom and have the creative urge of the inventor.

1 and 7: Should hold their own counsel and "paddle their own canoes" to eliminate conflict. Both must have the nerve to stand alone, with faith in themselves and their ideas.

6 and 2: Keep the atmosphere clear: For harmony, make known what you both want.

9 and 3: Quieting the emotions will be required: Carefully guard the tongue and there will be no problems for both of you.

8 and 4: Both wish mastery over their environment and must be mindful of each other's needs.

FIRST VOWELS IN NAMES

If you and your cat are to win each other's favor, observe the first vowel sound (A-E-I-O-U-Y-EW-OW) of the name most frequently used. The first vowel sound, especially of your cat's original name, shows instinctive reaction to outer stimuli. It registers emotional pulse and is even more dynamic when it is the first letter of the name rather than preceded by a consonant. For example, an "A" would be interested in a new idea, but if the "A" were preceded by a "D" or an "M" the individual would be more conservative, would want to know how much a thing was going to be worth, if it would work, etc.

A—These cats are responsive to new ideas, so long as they come from them. They are not in the least bit impressed by what you do or have. It does not matter what you want; they reserve the right to want something different. Old reliable routines antagonize them, but given an element of chance or something new to do, they will be very attentive.

E—They love variety. Their magnetism makes people want to pick them up, but they must have freedom, action, and frequent change. They are excellent judges of character and know how to ward off anything unpleasant. They convey the impression that you are really missing a thrilling adventure if you do not pick them up and stroke them. They are able to look both ways, at apparently the same time, like at the fridge door and the bedroom door.

I—The big idea is important to these cats, be it travel, ice cream,

or a cozy fire in the fireplace and no one to push them off the rug. They want the whole world, and scarcely less will satisfy. They cannot understand, when they give all the giving, why humans do not return the same and often stop stroking their neck after just an hour.

O—These cats like the responsibility of running the house their way. Although the humans still need some training, things appear to be going smoothly. Unfortunately humans still make loud or sudden noises, forget to leave doors open, and speak to cats in a high squeaky voice, as if they were deaf or stupid.

U—They are the light of the family, the joy of everyone's hearts. They are the ones you all look to when you need a pick-me-up, because they are wise; loving and playful; a connoisseur, a judge of character; an honest, conscientious, and tireless worker; someone who is always there, reliable and faultless. Or so you think.

Y—These cats have strong intuition and should heed it. They always appear to have something up their sleeve, to be holding something back, not revealing their true hand. Humans love this mysterious air—they invent all sorts of fantasies about royal breeding and pedigree just to make themselves feel good rubbing shoulders with these cats. But these cats do not cast their pearls before the uncouth. One must register a certain amount of perfection or depth of understanding before they will be drawn into bringing out the deep things they know. It is this love for penetrating the deeper whys and wherefores that gives them an authoritative knowledge and the respect that carries. They combine the qualities of 6 and 7, which makes 13, or 4. They know how to take a discussion and say nothing while blinking wisely. Of course they are analyzing and boiling it down into concrete facts. Then, if one stands the test of their measuring rule, one can depend on it: There is no more to be said.

EW as in "Lewis"—The diphthong here is composed of two 5s, making it a 10, or 1. These cats have the qualities of the "A" vowel to a certain extent. They are far more important to humans than humans are to them. In fact,

without working with them or through them, it would be difficult for humans to accomplish the larger things. If humans suffer because of these cats, it is just to teach them some vital lesson, for when they know how to handle (through the cat's teaching) each cat who crosses their path, their door to success will swing wide open.

OW as in "Brownie"—The diphthong of 6 and 5 makes 11, or 2, the inspirational quality that enables them to be a real light in their world. They have little patience with your shortcomings but will lead you to their point of view, so life should be much happier for both of you. These cats should not let others rule them, because if they do their 11 becomes a 2, and then, undecided as to what they should do, they will lose their inner poise and be compelled to shine only by the reflected light of a lesser mind. They belong in the limelight where, seeing their beam, others may take new courage from the stimulating, dynamic, penetrating, and almost hypnotic power that has been accorded them.

BIRTH DATE

The rhythm of greatest value is that of your cat's birth date, which directs the normal energy urge. All things in life are in rhythm with the basic notes of her birth date—sign, month, day, year, and final total all have some special meaning to your cat. Use the same process as for the name, reducing the year and all higher numbers to one single digit by adding the digits of the result.

For example, for a birth date of May 5, 1999, 5+5 (add month and day) to 1+9+9+9=38. Add 3+8 to get 11. Add 1+1 to get 2.

KEY TRAITS

The following is a list of the key character traits, according to the number value of your cat's name or birth date.

1—ambitious, autonomous, daring, heroic, winner

2—alert, analyst, attract, beauty, kind, steady, punctual, wise

3—absorbed, brave, friendly, good-natured, happy, observing

4—communicative, conscientious, fearless

5—awake early, brisk, explorer, intuition, power, waiting

6—absorbing, active, appealing, compassionate, decisive, benevolent

7—authoritative, courageous, dignified, polished, not secretive

8—anticipatory, tactful, sums up situation, open in communication

9—aesthetic sense, cool-headed, congenial, conquering, dazzling, often acting as if inspired

11—adventurer, agreeable, creative, independent, psychic

MUSIC, COLORS, FOODS, GEMS, AND FLOWERS

Cats are sensual, and so the joys of the senses—music, color, food, gems, and flowers—are special to them. Use your cat's birth date to find the things that bring your cat greatest joy and meaning. If you do not know the exact day of birth, then the birth or given name will suffice, although it is slightly less accurate. Birthdate indicates inherited characteristics, while the name reflects environmental influences.

MUSIC

Music, in the key of your cat's natal sign, may have a special appeal. Each sign is assigned a tone (see table). For instance, cats born in Aquarius (the eleventh sign) like especially the key of B♭—the eleventh tone of the octave. Strike the key of their natal sign on any instrument, or hum on this tone around them. This is the major note of their life song, their purr. They will build a chord up or down and hum their own melody. They do this to harmonize their inner and outer natures, and this makes them more at peace with themselves.

NATAL SIGN	TONE	COLOR
Aries (March 22–April 20)	C	Red
Taurus (April 21–May 21)	C#	Red/orange

NATAL SIGN	TONE	COLOR
Gemini (May 22–June 21)	D	Orange
Cancer (June 22–July 22)	E♭	Yellow/orange
Leo (July 23–August 23)	E	Yellow
Virgo (Aug 24–Sept 23)	F	Yellow/green
Libra (Sept 24–Oct 23)	F#	Green
Scorpio (Oct 24–Nov 21)	G	Blue/green
Sagittarius (Nov 22–Dec 21)	G#	Blue
Capricorn (Dec 22–Jan 20)	A	Blue/violet
Aquarius (Jan 21–Feb 19)	B♭	Violet
Pisces (Feb 20–March 21)	B	Red/violet

COLORS

Colors with the same vibration as the vowels of your cat's name may be in favor, but those in rhythm with the birth date total, then with the month, day, and year, are also significant. The same holds true for foods, gems, and flowers. A flower arrangement that includes a flower from each note of your cat's birth date would make an ideal color combination for your cat's cover or blanket.

The letters of the colors add to the number under which they appear. For example, using the chart on page 45, a-p-r-i-c-o-t is $1+7+9+9+3+6+2=37$, which is $3+7=10$, which is $1+0=1$.

1, 10—apricot, beige, crimson, flame, lilac, turquoise, red

2, 20—gold, salmon, bright orange

3—amber, orchid, yellow, rose

4—blue, emerald, green, indigo, green, cream

5—auburn, cherry, corn, lemon, pink, wisteria, blue

6—gray, henna, mulberry, peach, scarlet

7—brick, magenta, poppy, purple, violet

8—bronze, buff, canary, mauve, plum, tan

9—apple green, brown, lavender, red, sage

11—black, jade, violet, white, yellow

FOODS

Foods each have a numerological value. If the cat especially likes certain foods, then some link based on preference or nutritional need may be formed that correlates with its personality. The letters of the foods add to the number under which they appear:

1, 10—apricot, baked apple, baked beans, eggplant, halibut, jelly, lentils, meatloaf, olives, peanut butter, pumpkin, roast beef, salad, turkey

2, 20—breast of lamb, eggs, fowl, salmon

3—bread, cabbage, cobbler, grapes, liver, meat, peaches, pie, potatoes, prunes, toast, tomato

4—asparagus, buckwheat, carrots, cod, dates, eel, grapefruit, ham, honey, onion, parsnips, pineapple, pumpkin pie, sweetbreads

5—apple, bass, beet, broccoli, celery, corned beef, cucumber, endive, greens, lettuce, melon, onions, pears, tripe

6—apples, banana, beets, crab, fish, mushrooms, orange, peach, pork, potato, sole (flounder), spaghetti, sweet potato (kumara)

7—bananas, chops, fritters, herring, omelette, rhubarb, roast pork, scallops, shredded wheat, spinach

8—apple pie, bacon, baked potatoes, cauliflower, chicken, cottage cheese, custard pie,

raisins, rice, sardines, soup

9—beef, coleslaw, crabmeat, milk, orange juice, pastry, sweet potato pie, tomatoes, turnips, watermelon

11—baked potato, cake, clam, chestnut, shrimp, steak, tapioca, wild rice

GEMS AND STONES

The letters of the gems and stones add to the number under which they appear:

1, 10—lodestone, aquamarine, moss agate, turquoise

2, 20—gold

3—amber, amethyst, ruby, sardonyx

4—blood stone, emerald, moonstone, ochre, silver

5—brass, nephrite

6—diamond, jasper, marble, onyx, topaz

7—alabaster, agate, carat, pearl, platinum

8—bronze, beryl, chrysolite, crystal, mica, opal, pearls, scarab

9—nickel, opals

11—garnet, jacinth, jade, sapphire

FLOWERS AND TREES

The letters of the flowers and trees add to the number under which they appear:

1, 10—azalea, clematis, hollyhock, iris, lilac

2, 20—ivy, maple

3—daffodil, elm, honeysuckle, nasturtium, orchid, pansy, rose

4—fuschia, hemlock, pepper, sweet pea

5—carnation, gardenia, pink, primrose

6—chrysanthemum, dandelion, laurel, lotus, narcissus, palm, poplar, rosewood, tulip

7—fern, geranium, hyacinth, marigold, poppy, sunflower

8—begonia, dahlia, jasmine, rhododendron

9—buttercup, holly, magnolia, sycamore

11—chestnut, violet, weeping willow

A S T R O L O G Y

† H E Z O D i A C A Π D Y O U R C A †

The influence of each planet and its dominance over the lives of all living beings has been used from the times of the Chaldean civilization in the ancient land of Ur up to the present day. The stars and the signs each have a different influence on all living beings. It is the vibration of these that causes a cat to be fast or slow, calm or energetic, depending on the force.

The zodiac signs that guide astrological readings are the following:

Aries—March 21–April 19

Taurus—April 20–May 20

Gemini—May 21–June 21

Cancer—June 22–July 22

Leo—July 23–August 23

Virgo—August 24–September 23

Libra—September 24–October 23

Scorpio—October 24–November 22

Sagittarius—November 23–December 21

Capricorn—December 22–January 19

Aquarius—January 20–February 18

Pisces—February 19–March 20

Loviπg Harmoπy

How strong the harmony is between you and your cat can be found in astrological readings. Venus, Mars, Jupiter, Uranus, Neptune, and the Moon play a big part in the love nature between you and your cat. A brief outline of what they mean to the cat will give you an idea of what to expect from your cat and what to look for in choosing a cat. Date of birth is once again the decisive piece of information required.

In your cat's horoscope, Venus controls the material nature of love, the kind of love your cat is capable of, the place where it might see it, and how it will go about getting it.

The power to intensify the cat's physical expression of how much it loves you is due to the character and position of Mars in the birth chart. Mars can even make cats quite forceful in showing their love by mistakenly scratching you, constantly following you, and rubbing themselves against your leg.

Although Jupiter has many other far-reaching influences in the average chart, there are positions where it can greatly enhance opportunities. In a female cat's horoscope, the Moon in friendly relationship to Jupiter can indicate a very long-lasting cat-owner bond.

Uranus indicates a deep, powerful magnetism between the two natures when occupying the same degree and sign position as the Moon in your birth chart.

The position and quality of Neptune in the birth chart gives emotions to the affectional nature. The Moon has a decided effect on every cat's bonding fate. Many of the other qualities that make for good emotional appeal are made by the blend of Neptune and Venus or Neptune and the Moon.

SIGN GROUPINGS

The first step toward choosing a cat who will be affectionate towards you is by comparing the sun sign. The fire signs are all harmonious to each other, and the same rule applies to the air, earth, and water signs.

Aries, Leo, and Sagittarius cats are happy to share their love with more than one person. They share the same basic natures: warm, loyal, easy-natured, and love for the affection of humans. Several of the other elements blend very well, and the harmonious combinations for the fire signs are as follows:

Aries cats are well aspected to Gemini and Aquarius owners of the air trinity. The awareness of these airy personalities appeals to energetic Aries cats.

Leo cats get a good response from Libra and Gemini. The innate taste, high-bred appearance, and natural good breeding of the Libra cat often seeks an owner who keeps the home immaculate.

The Sagittarian personality of the cat could find great companionship with either Aquarius or Libra. The Aquarian intellect and caring nature are very sympathetic to the Sagittarian cat, and the unconventional Aquarian would greatly enjoy the playful, energetic Sagittarian cat.

Cats and humans born in the air trinity make harmonious companions for each other. As shown, the air signs harmonize well with the fire signs, and particular divisions of each class create good companions for each other.

The earth trinity—Taurus, Virgo and Capricorn—are in harmony. These signs get along extremely well with humans who have the same sign and show loyalty and affection.

Taurus cats blend quite well with people who are Cancer and Pisces, more especially the male Taurus cat with a female Cancer or Pisces owner. All three groups are affectionate and agreeable.

The Capricorn cat will have an excellent relationship with its Pisces owner. This combination is even stronger with a female Capricorn cat and a male Pisces owner. The Capricorn is known for its great strength. Owners would be able to be away all day knowing

that their cat would not sit at home all day waiting. The warmth and devotion of the Pisces owner would infuse happiness into the life of a Capricorn cat.

Scorpio owners are also good for the Capricorn cat. The Scorpio owner is often protective of the cat, and the frugal virtues of the Capricorn cat would satisfy the owner's expectations that the cat will be loyal and affectionate, remaining close to the Scorpian owner.

Those in the water trinity are considered harmonious with one another: Pisces, Scorpio, and Cancer. Most of the other signs harmonizing well with the water trinity have already been mentioned. The possible exception is a Cancer cat with a Virgo owner. The Cancer cat is a loving, whimsical, and inside cat and would put great trust in the Virgo owner. The Virgo owner is adequate from the viewpoint of affections for the Cancer cat.

THE ROLE OF VENUS

Regardless of actual birth sign, in order to find what love your cat has for you, you need to know in what sign Venus was positioned at the cat's birth, using the kitten's birth date.

Aries: The pace and energy of Aries is fast and full of life, compared to the material character of Venus. Because Venus's domestic leanings are not encouraged by Aries, these cats like to show signs of worldly accomplishment, such as catching birds and mice. The fast pace of Aries makes them quick-witted and ready for action, and the material character of Venus makes them want to show off their prey to you.

Taurus: Venus is very powerful in Taurus. It is the ruler of the sign, and cats with Venus in Taurus are at their happiest when they have material things around them, such as blankets, their own chair to sit in, and toys with which to play. These things will make them very happy, and they will show you great love and affection. There is a determined urge toward domestic contentment and the satisfaction of knowing that they are in a safe and loving environment.

At times they can be ruthless and pushy to get what they want in their quest for love and the material good things of life. The love nature is deep, secret, and unchanging.

Gemini: Venus is moderately strong in Gemini. These cats love food, warmth, or companionship and do not hold back on showing you affection. They like to play games and can be full of fun and mischief.

Cancer: Venus has a very maternal quality in Cancer. These cats will seek love and affection through their ability to mother and protect, quite often making sure you are not out of their sight line. They will often sleep very close to you, even under the sheets. They seek love with everybody who comes into the household, although still remaining loyal to you. The love of these cats is very deep, protective, and nourishing.

Leo: The sign of Leo is a very strong sign, so that any planet found positioned there at birth will have a good deal of energy. Leo-Venus cats are generous in showing affection towards humans. The nature of Leo is arid, like the sun, and planets coming under this dominion reflect something of its character. Cats having Venus posited in Leo achieve their need for being constantly patted, picked up, and cuddled by humans through their own efforts and force of personality. They are rich in the magnetism to attract humans to them.

Virgo: Venus is not as strong in Virgo, making these cats rather timid in a group of strangers. However, they are very loyal and loving to humans they know and are comfortable with.

Libra: Venus is at the peak of her power in Libra, being ruler of this sign. Cats who have her positioned in Libra at birth make the most interesting and lovable cats of all types. These cats are often well-bred, and their whole behavior of seeking love and affection is one of gracious appreciation. These cats are among the most affection-seeking of all types and will often do the strangest and funniest things to get it. Those cats who are more happily balanced make the most desirable, if not the most affectionate, cats in the zodiac.

Scorpio: Venus is at her very weakest in Scorpio. The Scorpio nature often overrides the force of Venus, making these cats very independent yet also extremely devoted and generous. These cats will often show off by climbing trees and catching birds and mice to win your affection.

Sagittarius: The relationship between this sign and Venus is friendly, although Venus is only moderately powerful in the sign. These cats seek love by letting you know what they want by meowing. They often end up living in very well-to-do homes and understand your voice.

Capricorn: Venus is not at her best in this sign, making these very individual cats. Their needs are mostly food and warmth, and if you provide these they will be very happy. At times they can be timid and lack confidence in approaching humans but are quite happy exploring new places and will wander to a neighbor's home in search of adventure.

Aquarius: The position of Venus in the birth chart often makes what is described as a "highbrow" cat: one who often displays intelligence and taste in life. They will be happy if they have the best of everything. They desire human companionship and harmony in the household.

Pisces: Venus is exalted in Pisces and in one of her most powerful positions in the zodiac. Here Venus is in her own element, combined with a sign that expands her lush qualities. This Neptunian Venus makes these cats a little wary of humans at first, but they will more often than not slowly like and finally love them. Very devoted, they often express their love by heavy purring. The females are better suited to the quality of the position than are male cats. The softness of the temperament is naturally feminine. Cats of this type carry an indefinable aura of love and affection in their appearance and manner.

YOUR CAT'S HOROSCOPE

After the general rules offered for the best harmony between you and your cat and the additional personality information added by the position of Venus in the signs, it will be helpful to read an analysis of the cats created by the sign characters of the zodiac. Find your cat's sign from the date divisions given earlier, then read the suggestions for a better understanding of your cat.

Note that there are subtle differences between male and female cats, which will be pointed out in the sections that follow. There is also a separate entry for kittens. During the early years of the kitten's life, the influence of the planetary nativity is quite strong, as the experiences of life plus the profession of heavenly transits have not had a chance to alter the original pattern. The kitten entry, therefore, will give you some idea of the kitten's fundamental makeup.

ARIES

The symbol for this sign is the Ram, a powerful animal with considerable grandeur. The Ram usually gets its way and may achieve its goal by using its awesome power. Aries would not be afraid to use its power to get what it wants.

Aries represents the head of the cat body. The purpose and chief focus of the Aries cat is to be near a family and feel wanted. Aries has a powerful, unconscious drive to add to or alter the biological gene pool of its kittens, which drives them to look for cats of different make-up to breed with, thereby producing offspring who are smarter, stronger, usually larger, and better adapted to survive in the future than the norm.

Aries is the pioneer and adventurer and is highly energetic, making things happen. Known for its courage, it likes to think it is the best at what it does.

The ruler of Aries is Mars, the planet of hard work and accomplishment. This will make your cat want to spend time outdoors and

release some of its energy. There is an instinct with the Mars force for the cat to be playful with other cats.

Female: Some signs of the zodiac, regardless of whether they are masculine or feminine signs, make better feminine cats than masculine. Aries is a very masculine sign, but the Aries male cats are not often pure types, and then much of the strength of the sign is dissipated. Female Aries cats make wonderful companions and pets for the working owner. They are very independent and healthy and are able to find shelter easily. They are easily pleased and are as happy to be alone in the sun during the day as they are with mixed company in the household at night. They are usually good-looking cats and very clean. When other cats are present, this female Aries cat will often make the others jealous. She will also be very territorial and not welcome other cats onto her patch. This type of cat is at her happiest with owners who show her great affection and love.

Male: The Aries male cat, when found somewhat near the pure type, is a very distinguished cat. This cat has many appealing qualities, including good temperament and a cute face. Very fussy, everything needs to be in its correct place, such as the food bowl or cushion where he usually sleeps. They prefer more mature owners who are stable and quite often set in their ways. If something is out of line, this male Aries cat will be quite vocal about it until it is changed. He considers it a personal affront that he should have to look outside of his home for affection, but he can be rather demanding in gaining love from you, and if he is not gratified, he will let you know.

Kitten: The most precocious and lively of the signs, the Aries kitten should be discouraged from a tendency to show off because they may become very demanding. These kittens are proud, so don't hurt their feelings by making fun of them. A certain amount of freedom will do these kittens good, if only for the mistakes they will make, and they should be encouraged at times to guide themselves.

TAURUS

The Bull is the symbol for Taurus. Taurus represents the throat in the cat body. Cats who have a very songlike quality to their meow are often Taurus cats.

Taurus's whole purpose in life is to be needed and comfortable in a household, which is one of the reasons Taureans are the second most wealthy of the astrology signs in terms of having comfort from their owners. Taurus likes luxury and open space and is also very sexual.

Venus, the ruler of Taurus, colors this cat's appearance and personality. This explains why your cat can attract other cats and is popular.

Female: The female Taurus cat is perhaps the most devoted and dependable kind of cat. She will endure extreme hardship rather than desert you. Naturally, when making this statement, the devotion of the Cancer female cat and the Leo female cat rises up to contest the assertion. Nonetheless, the Taurus cat has a nature peculiarly adapted to domestic life. She is the perfect house cat, a devoted pet who is easily satisfied. These cats are often calm and will easily become everybody's friend. She will rarely stray from home. She is a very affectionate, demonstrative cat, wholly engrossed in her home. She makes herself very dependent, although she can really help herself if necessary. These devoted cats are best with a caring type of owner who talks to them and spends time playing with them, giving them attention and love.

Male: The male Taurus cat has the finest qualities of all of the signs for being a great companion. He makes a devoted pet, dependable, faithful, and trusting of his owners. He adores his owners and strains to express this

affection. These cats often end up with owners above their station in life, partly because of their desire to be cared for and partly because their worldly nature leads them toward higher social owners. To hold on to the love and affection of the male Taurus cat, you must always show a great deal of love towards him. These cats also love dependence and always like to feel that they are part of the family.

Kitten: One of the most playful and beautiful kittens of the zodiac, they are usually well-grown, developed, sturdy, and healthy in appearance. These kittens respond to love and affection and crave a great deal of petting. Their apparent stolidness is really insecurity, and this will vanish if they are encouraged to be friendly from a young age. A tendency towards self-indulgence means these cats can easily become lazy, but gentle interest and quiet stimulation will bring to life all of their fine qualities.

GEMINI

Symbolized by the Twins, Gemini is an air sign. Gemini represents the front paws, arms, and lungs in the cat body. All the air signs have the sense of intellect and change. Their gift is understanding the consequences of change, which sometimes is as important as the change itself. Planning, waiting, and analyzing information is what the air signs do best.

Gemini's purpose is to bring peace and harmony to the planet. These cats are often highly intelligent, and you are not

mistaken if you think your cat understands everything you say.

Mercury, the ruler of intellect, is the ruler of Gemini. The intellectual force and smart co-ordination of body make this a very agile cat. Mercury controls the quick thinking of the cat, which is expressed in its reflexes.

Female: This type of cat is a very intellectual cat in the world of cats. She greatly needs to be part of the family and sleeps indoors. During the day this cat will often seek entertainment outside the house, and it is important she is not kept housebound. Female Gemini cats are particular about what time they are fed and go to sleep; they like things to run to clockwork.

Male: These cats enjoy their own company and are very adventurous. You can go away knowing that your cat will not be wondering when you are going to return. These cats enjoy the outdoor life and, if you spend a lot of time in the garden, the cat will not be far behind, chasing leaves, watching birds, or wandering around the yard.

Kitten: Gemini kittens are, like the dual sign, both a blessing and a problem. They are energetic, often showing artistic ability very early on. Their weakness is in their disposition: They can be nervous, highly strung kittens who find it hard to rest or sleep, both of which are necessary for their health and well-being. Their desire to meow had best be quietly curbed—although cute in a kitten, later in life it may develop into constant meowing and whining. If the kitten is not affectionate, this can be overcome by tenderness and loving demonstrations.

CANCER

Symbolized by the Crab, Cancer represents the stomach and breast in the cat body. Cancer represents the principle of individual survival in the world. Cancer is food and love, the two parts of basic survival. Thus, Cancer's favorite room is the kitchen. They are also very sensitive and sometimes psychic.

Cancer is represented by the Moon, which deals with the mood of your cat and governs the way your cat can adjust to its surroundings. Cancer is usually the wealthiest of all the zodiac signs with respect to affection. The Cancer cat can live equally well with just one owner or with a family.

Female: The female Cancer cat follows you constantly and is very motherly towards you. She typifies the most motherly influence of all of the zodiacal female cats. When at her best, she is affectionate, protective of any young children or other animals, devoted to you, adaptable, and easily satisfied. She is very comfortable making her home anywhere. There is no need to have a special chair for her or her own food bowl, for example. She realizes that her devotion to you will get her love and warmth in return. All this, of course, depends upon the planetary combinations in nativity.

Male: This cat is known for his easygoing nature. The recessive male Cancer cat is very passive and lazy, and he will be happy to lie in one spot all day and not move. These cats prefer owners who will give them domestic comfort. They have a deeply traditional love for being in one home all their life and share many of the qualities imputed to the female Cancer cat. He is devoted to the family, and his whole mind will be wrapped up in you and your family, although his disposition is such that these feelings are translated into exacting demands for food and attention. These cats love constant human closeness.

Kitten: Cancer kittens are like sensitive plants. More often than not they have none of the graces found in some of the other signs: They are not as clever, talented, or even robust. They are more likely to be fanciful, moody, clinging little things, hungering for love and understanding. They get strange passionate attachments for humans and absorb almost anything that attracts them, and so they must be encouraged towards a more active and independent lifestyle. They are very receptive early on, so plenty of activity is important to bring out their natural manual dexterity. Their health is exceedingly delicate and their appetite poor, but a happy family life with routine and plenty of affection, love, and playfulness will promote the best development.

LEO

Leo's symbol is the Lion, the King of Beasts. Leo is associated with the heart and back in the cat body. Leo is in constant motion and very proud. They enjoy being around family and being the center of attention. These cats are often very playful and enjoy children.

Governed by the Sun, Leo is constantly burning and highly energetic, wanting to be center stage in life. They are performers.

Female: The female Leo cat is a splendid type of cat for a worldly, ambitious owner. She is very well behaved and easy to look after. She is very quick and a good hunter and enjoys all human company. She attracts a lot of attention from people and is gentle-natured. The love of a female Leo cat is enduring and self-sacrificing. These are the most loyal of female cats, whose whole lives are lived through their deep lovable

natures. Paired with owners who are go-getters in life, all of her good qualities will be reduced to their rightful proportions. No human being could repay the Leo cat's devotion to her owner and household.

Male: The male Leo cat fits into the scheme of domestic life quite smoothly. He is tremendously proud and often demands center stage. He is very affectionate, loving, and loyal, but he will not tolerate any person who ill-treats him. The average Leo male cat makes a good family cat, as he is very safe around young children, and his tolerance makes him very good for the owner who loves cats.

Kitten: Leo kittens are the most vital and active. Highly strung, domineering, and much inclined to show off, they are often very cute and good-looking kittens, lovable and full of energy. They excel in mice catching and are healthy, tireless, and able to compete successfully in any field where other cats are the contenders. Unfortunately, this means that if they are unrestrained, they can be much too bossy and demanding and want their own way. This kitten offers a rich nature of good impulses, but because of the vast amount of energy, it needs very careful direction.

VIRGO

Virgo is represented by the planet Mercury, making this cat a quick thinker and mover. Their symbol is the Virgin, the symbol of the harvest. Virgo represents the intestines in the cat body. Virgo is social or group-oriented, enjoying mingling with humans.

Female: The female Virgo cat makes an excellent pet. She is extremely clean and likes a regular routine (for example, to be fed at the same time each day and let out at night at the same time). She is also very efficient and just as capable outdoors as she is indoors. The female Virgo cat is apt to be fussy about which humans she lets pat her and will guard her space with the utmost vigilance. She makes a very loyal cat and is protective of you.

Male: These male cats seem to accept domesticity because it is part of the world's social scheme. In many cases, he enjoys his own space and companionship. Like the Virgo female, he is capable of providing for himself, but if he is going to be fed by humans he, too, enjoys regularity and things to run like clockwork. This cat safeguards his home and is careful to protect it. He makes friends with humans easily and enjoys being around groups of people.

Kitten: Virgo kittens are one of the most mental types of the twelve signs. Although happy to lie in the sun and daydream, they are very curious and will try to get into everything —an open drawer, an open cupboard — and will climb the highest tree to see what is at the top. Their problem is disposition: They have an urge toward everything being just right, but in the search they become cross, peevish, and irritable. The basis of all this is an inherent lack of warmth and a coldness toward humanity, so be especially affectionate, but in a manner that is not too physical, with gentle, tender stroking. If sociability is encouraged early in life, much of this squeamishness will disappear as the cat matures.

LIBRA

Libra is represented by the planet Venus and is symbolized by blind Justice. An air sign, Libra is represented by a humanlike symbol. Libra is associated with the kidneys in the cat body.

Libra is the family air sign and so subconsciously wants to be in a stimulating family environment. Libra cats are creative, idealist, and artistic. They are the most attractive of the zodiac.

Female: One of the most interesting natures is found in either sex of the Libra cat. This sign has a decided feminine leaning, with the highest Venus influence prevailing. These cats have a delicate, spiritual appeal. They are ideal cats for wealthy, successful owners. She often has an exotic look about her and quite often looks deceptively fragile. The Libra female cat is a fine companion and well able to bring harmony into the home life. She has an instinctive knowledge of how to get along with people, at the same time never neglecting your needs, but giving them all the loving attention of which her gracious nature is capable. The Libra female cat is distinctly a luxury.

Male: The Libra cat is a caring cat, a respecter of humans and their ways. You will not often find the Libra male mixing with other cats

relying on their owner and will fret if the owner is not there for them all the time. With the Libra kitten especially, a good deal of responsibility for how the kitten grows rests with you.

SCORPIO

Ruled by Mars, the Scorpio cat is courageous and strong. Scorpio has three symbols, the only astrology sign to have more than one symbol. The best-known symbol is the Scorpion, but the Eagle and the Serpent also are, or have been, used in many ancient cultures to symbolize Scorpio. Scorpio relates to the sex organs of the cat body. Scorpio represents family survival or perpetuation of the species through the act of mating and is legendary for sexual prowess. Scorpio cats are intense and very energetic.

Female: The female Scorpio cat is a very primitive type, and her deep cat instincts are aroused by the different functions of being a pet. The best Scorpio female cats are loyal and courageous, needing not too many home comforts to keep her at home. She enjoys human contact and being around a lot of mixed company. Once she is settled with you, she becomes rather lazy in nature and tends not to jump fences, climb trees, or chase birds. She will often be quite happy to sit and watch the world

because he prefers the company of humans. No other cat in the zodiac can order life with so much wisdom. His superior agility and quick-mindedness are his greatest virtues. However, if he were to see you patting another cat or animal he would be very hurt.

Kitten: Libra kittens are not simple personalities to develop. Both clinging and reserved, they crave love but have so much restraint that it is hard for them to relax. Often skittish, they can be good tree climbers and hunters if they can overcome their apathetic disposition. As far as cats go, they are supremely unambitious, and so from early in the kitten's life the owner must encourage them to fend for themselves. If they do not cultivate such self-direction, they will grow up go by. The difference in the atmosphere of her surroundings lies in the intensity of her feelings. She is fearless and will take nonsense from nobody. She will accept her surroundings and make the most of them. She is neither shy, diffident, nor tactful in getting the things she wants, such as food when she wants it. She expresses herself with the greatest force and requires vigorous attention on demand, quite often pushing her head hard against your body.

Male: The male Scorpio cat is the typical "old-fashioned lord of the manor" type of cat who is happy in any room of the house. He is often very well balanced and will be able to live with a family very well if he so desires. He makes a very devoted family pet and can never

get enough love and attention. The depths of his affection for you are genuine.

Kitten: Among the most active and energetic of kittens, they have good, naturally inquisitive minds and are full of fun. Their capacity for adventure is tremendous, and their nature is rich in avenues for development. Difficulties lie in their character, however. Scorpio kittens will often use persuasion to get their own way—and if they cannot get their own way by fair means, they will find another way. Selfishness and self-indulgence are strong in the Scorpio kitten's nature, and you will have your hands full in combating the evils lying dormant in their nature. If you do your work well, the kitten will have a happier life when grown up.

SAGITTARIUS

Sagittarius is related to the planet Jupiter, whose personality is fun loving, generous, and gentle. Symbolized by the Centaur (half man, half horse), Sagittarius is associated with the thighs of the cat body. Sagittarius wants to reform human society by using its animal instincts. They are impatient crusaders, calling their many reforming beliefs from the rooftops. Sagittarius is the spiritual cat leader of the zodiac, being very "high-minded." They also

71

love travel. They are likely to be very social, energetic, of higher consciousness, and may subscribe to the theory of Oneness in the Universe.

Female: The female Sagittarius cat is the best fitted of all zodiacal types to be a companion for humans. She takes an interest in you and will quite often follow you—she is one of the few cats who can travel well in a car, so long as she is being held by you. She is not an intruder in the household routine and has enough reserve to wait for her dinner or to go outside. She loves the outdoors and enjoys hunting, chasing leaves and other things. She has a very inquisitive nature about her. You do not have to search for companionship too much—she is very energetic, fun-loving, warm, and friendly, and enjoys trying different things; you can have a very full life with such a companion. In the home, she is easy to care for and is quite happy to be by herself some of the time. A good percentage of athletic agility goes with this birth position, and these cats are often rather big and smartly groomed. They can demand an active life at times, for there is nothing of the languid hothouse bloom about them. There is no jealousy in their nature and they get along well with most other cats of compatible signs. The

emotional nature of the female Sagittarius cat is highly nervous.

Male: The male Sagittarius cat requires a wise, patient, and caring owner. This may be true of all owners, but the male cats born with this birth figure have much to give. Frequently your family, because you will not cater to innate peculiarities of the male cat, sees the worst side of the character rather than the best. He loves the outdoors, open space, and fresh air, and can be quite a wanderer. You need to be exceedingly broad-minded, free from jealousy, and impersonal, even if this is not natural for you. The male Sagittarian cat will stay with you for a long time and makes a good pet. These are clever and loving cats, with whom it is a privilege to live. However, because of his impatience with anything ordered in his life, you will need to widen your own horizon on your views of what pets need.

Kitten: These kittens are usually a joy to their owners. Happy, full of life and fun, with a natural tendency toward good behavior, Sagittarian kittens tend to choose the right rather than the wrong way to do things. They are full of love and affection for humans and, consequently, are popular. This leads to its own problems, however, because the Sagittarian all through life suffers from an excess of trust in humankind. The Sagittarian kitten rebels against control, is willful and tries to throw off your authority, so wherever possible, allow them freedom of action. They love being outside and running around and should be encouraged to play outside.

CAPRICORN

Capricorn is represented by the planet Saturn. They are symbolized by the Goat, which is stubborn, eats almost anything, and likes established order. Capricorn represents the tail in the cat body.

Female: The female Capricorn cat is rather masculine in her appearance and temperament.

Routine to her is a joy, with a basic need in her own mind to make sure she still feels wanted by you. She is loyal to the nth degree and will follow you to the end of the earth. She is really an admirable kind of cat, needing most of all affection to call forth all her deep loyalty, which once given lasts a lifetime. Owners who often go away and have others look after their pets will find this type of cat very satisfactory.

Male: The male Capricorn cat falls in readily enough with the domestic scheme, enjoying relaxing in the sun or in a warm spot most of the time. He appears to be happy around most people, but his basic nature is selfish. He is a very good mouser and often wants to show off his winnings to you as a way of getting more

attention. This cat is very curious and will examine whatever he gets, such as food and toys. Naturally, the harsh tone that this birth figure casts over a personality is usually tempered by the other configurations—in which case many of the sober Capricorn qualities are embellished by softer moods, making a much more agreeable cat.

Kitten: Capricorn kittens are mature for their age, solemn, repressed, and unresponsive—so work hard to lighten the darkness of this temperament. These kittens are rather slow in their mental responses, but they are exceedingly painstaking and persevering. They do not have naturally sweet dispositions, and you will have to work very hard to eradicate tendencies toward deceit and spitefulness. If you detect such tendencies, treat them like a physical illness and you will slowly and patiently develop trust and sweetness in their stead.

AQUARIUS

Aquarius is represented by the planet of freedom, Uranus. The vibration given off by Uranus suggests connection on an advanced plane. Aquarius, being an air sign, is symbolized by a humanlike figure, the Water Bearer. Carrying water is a uniquely human act, done

to ensure personal survival—this makes the Aquarius cat very adaptable. Moving drinking water from one place to another is an act of intellect and one that shows thoughtful preparation for the future. Aquarius represents the ankles and the blood in the cat body.

Female: The female Aquarian cat is one of the highest of the zodiacal types. She is very well-equipped for being with large numbers of humans, in that she is very capable and adaptable. She often maintains an interest in chasing and climbing trees all through her life. Like the female Sagittarian cat, she makes a very fine companion. Female Aquarian cats are the friendliest in the world, and they would rather suffer themselves than create a condition in the home that might bring her owner grief and sorrow. If she is about to die of natural causes, for example, she will often run away.

Male: The male Aquarian cat is the kindest and most generous of all the types. He is not overbearing or constantly seeking human touch, unless some other planetary configurations stimulate this urge. However, being gracious and kindly, he accepts being looked after by humans as part of the domestic scheme of the world and, cooperative as he is, makes a great success of it, leaning towards great harmony in the home. He thrives on the closeness of human touch and, because of his temperament, gets along well with strangers. It has been said that the Aquarian's universal nature will one day be the attitude of the entire cat population. In the meantime, the domestic life of such cats will be far more successful if they have owners who enjoy talking to their cats and keeping them stimulated.

Kitten: These kittens are very promising in many ways. They are not highly intellectual, but they have a great interest in progressive accomplishment and even in their home. An Aquarian kitten of either sex, but especially the male, has a distinctly caring and affection-ate trend. They want to make you as happy as possible and think very little about themselves. Aquarian kittens have a strong sense of obligation to you and exert themselves to be worthy of trust.

PISCES

Pisces is associated with the planet Neptune, making this a rather mystical and affectionate cat. Fish swimming in opposite directions while in reeds symbolize Pisces, which explains why some people think of Pisceans as confused. Pisces is associated with the paws of the cat body. The Pisces cat is very sensitive and aware of its surroundings. Pisces may be the stray cat or the cat who helps the stray cat

because they represent the "street" side of life. They often have artistic abilities and enjoy listening to music.

Female: The female Pisces cat is ideally adapted for domestic life. She is not as active as many of the other types, nor as capable of fending for herself. She would not be found for example, living by herself in the streets, rather she would be with other cats who can look after her. Not that the Pisces female cat is incompetent, for she herself has a great sense of comfort and is caring in nature, but feeling safe and having a home that is stable is a luxurious place of refuge. Sometimes the health of the female Pisces cat is delicate, and then it takes the utmost strength of will to keep her from getting depressed. You can best do this by making a fuss over her, feeding her extra little treats, and providing an extra warm blanket at night during the cold winter months. This negative side of the sensitive Pisces nature is not inviting, but when the type is more robust the female makes the most kind-natured, loving, and devoted of cats. She is extremely responsive to affection, which tends to make her a very good pet for young children.

Male: The male Pisces cat is full of doubtful benefits to the household of humans. He is one of the most loving and attentive of male cats. He spends more time indoors than any other type, save perhaps the male Cancer cat, but he is not good at showing his need for affection. He will often spend most of this time asleep or dreaming. His notions, dreams, and misconceptions are more real to him than the difficulties of living or catching food if need be. Such difficulties are almost impossible to conquer, and therefore are immediately substituted by him with a phantom world. He will seek sympathetic response to his physical nature.

Kitten: This kitten has great potential for good. They are deeply spiritual kittens, always wishing for the perfect and the beautiful. Although lacking self-confidence, these cats can often show talent, making the best bird catchers. They are always certain that they cannot compete with other kittens and shrink from the pain of failure; consequently, they would much rather not try at all. This is why they often seem lazy, spending most of their time watching the world go by. Owners need to induce a sense of fun and play and encourage the kitten to go and catch a mouse and show it off to them. It is true that life is difficult, but not nearly as hard as it appears to the Piscean. The wise owner will instill self-confidence in this kitten.

MOOD CHANGES AND THE ZODIAC

Owners want to know why one minute their cats appear friendly and cuddly, and the next minute they are scratching them. Like humans, cats have mood changes. Many of us know when our cat is suffering from a passing mood, because they sometimes seem rather depressed. Others, unaware that their cats are victims of emotional manipulation, try to make their cats live a routine life, rather than see to their special needs.

Certain astrological types of acts are receptive subjects for moods, fears, and worries. Naturally there are degrees of susceptibility, and the birth chart determines which of the sun signs make the cat succumb more readily to aspects of fear and worry as life advances.

It is very hard to unbalance cats born in the sign of Aquarius, Leo, Taurus, or Scorpio. Their natural makeup gives them qualities that withstand the fast-paced human world. In the case of Aquarius, superior mental equipment and selflessness disarm fright. But with Leo it is a kingly sense of power and safety and the conviction of inner strength, and with Taurus it is a solid effort of will and earthy strength against the unseen. Scorpios bring to the forefront their uncanny understanding of the unknown. Scorpio cats are not troubled by the forces of darkness or the pull of impulsive behavior. This is the most occult of the signs and these cats have an innate understanding of moods and impulses.

The signs of Aries, Libra, and Capricorn come next in the strength to throw off worry and fear. The signs of Gemini, Virgo, Sagittarius, Cancer, and Pisces, however, are the weakest and most susceptible to aspects of threatened disaster. This is because they are "mutable signs," meaning inconstant and capable of or susceptible to change. The exception is Cancer, which although not a mutable sign, is ruled by the Moon, whose influence gives a variable, changeable, timid nature that certainly leans toward fear and worry.

Therefore, Aquarius, Leo, Taurus, and Scorpio cats can control worry and anxiety during their lives. Cats born in the signs of Aries, Libra, and Capricorn find the strength to fight moods and fears, but the cats with birthdays in Gemini, Virgo, Sagittarius, Cancer, and Pisces succumb to the demons of the blues. To know this is a large part of winning the battle: If your cat belongs to a susceptible sign, its troubles seem overpowering and, like shadows, are greatly magnified and often entirely unreal.

The astral influences that create worry, depression, and fears are Saturn, Neptune, Mars, and the Moon. Venus and Jupiter, on the other hand, provide positive, optimistic influences. If one of the four depressing planets are afflicted in the nativity, the cat is a natural-born worrier: It will worry about affection, food, warmth, and so on. Even if this is not the case, unfavorable aspects to the cat's sun and other natal and progressed positions mean that it will be temporarily affected. You have two options. The first is to force the unwilling spirit of the cat into action and, knowing the mood is a false one, play with them more and communicate your own happy disposition. The second is to let the cat behave as though it is living in a dream, and upon wakening take up the thread of action.

Saturn is the greatest single influence in the zodiac in creating false fears and exaggerated terrors. If Saturn is positioned in Gemini, Virgo, Sagittarius, or Pisces at birth, the cat will be subject to dour moods and an exaggerated concept of danger. The cycle of Saturn is approximately twenty-eight years, the time it takes the planet to make the complete circle of the zodiac. The critical periods of Saturn come every seven years, when it is in square aspect, opposition, or transiting the sign in which the cat was born. When it is making the two-and-one-half-year transit of the cat's birth sign, the mood can be one of great depression and discouragement. This cat will lack energy and just lie around. Extra rest, discipline, and determination not to let the cat give in to self-pity will help maintain poise through this period.

The Moon is perhaps the best known of all the makers of moods. From the New Moon through the waxing crescent to the first quarter, the cat is fanciful, apprehensive, and a worrier all its life.

Since the Moon passes swiftly through the signs, the phases of the moon act as a messenger of mood. The nature of the Moon is absorbing, reflective, and retentive. In this passage from signs they release as well as collect. Some of the collected influences are dispersed in transit, and other qualities are absorbed for future release. Consequently, every cat is subject to a variety of changing impulses and moods, unreasonable and often unexplainable. The energy dispersed by the Moon accounts for the mood of the moment—the swift change of thought, often irrational, sometimes intuitive, but all of it founded on the lunar tides. This ebb and flow of activity is an important function of the Moon astrologically because it is the ruler of cat energy. Periods of rest, inactivity, quiet, and inertia come during the decrease of the Moon. With the full moon comes action, agitation, and a general release of violent energy. With this outward flow of life comes a climax: It may be good or bad, according to the nature of the planets coloring the lunar tide.

The Moon controls all the fluids of the body and this includes the adrenal glands. When the Moon is waning, the cat's body fluids are at low ebb, and weariness, depression, and melancholia result. With a full moon comes the return of vitality. Should the action of Venus or Jupiter govern this lunar tide, a vast release of optimism, joy, and constructive energy results. Jupiter, of all the planets, brings hope and good.

THE ZODIAC AND THE OWNER

We are only now beginning to realize how badly equipped most of us are to be good pet owners. We are discovering how little we have understood the cat's delicate nature and how much damage we have been doing to the growing personality of the kitten, which, with a little intelligent preparation, might be better equipped to face the struggle for existence. Among the astrological types, some of us are naturally suited to be cat owners, while astrology can point out to others where they may be failing and can suggest how they may improve.

ARIES

The Aries owner of either sex is kind and generous to cats but not always sympathetic or understanding of their needs. This is particularly true of the male Aries owner, who, although proud of his cat, is apt to be impatient, irritable, and unwilling to see things from the cat's point of view. The female Aries owner is a somewhat different personality. She too is intensely proud of her cat and apt to be somewhat unconventional and advanced in her methods of bringing up a kitten. She may urge her cats to catch mice and birds and show off their prey, and of course it depends upon the astrological group of her cat whether this is a good thing or not. It is always good to encourage cats to develop their natural instincts rather than override them. On the whole, barring impatience, Aries owners, and particularly Aries female owners, are fairly efficient and a good example of independence and courage to the growing kitten.

TAURUS

Taurus owners of either sex are often considered one of the ideal types of owners. They have endless patience and a natural love for animals and the home life, which so often revolves around youngsters and pets. This routine is not boring to the Taurean as it is to so many of the other zodiacal types. Taureans almost always choose country life, or at least suburban life, which is ideal for cats. Owners of this group have a very protective instinct and, although they are seldom brilliant intellectually themselves, their kindness of heart towards their cats goes a long way to giving the cats the kind of lives they most desire.

Gemini

Gemini owners of either sex do not make ideal cat owners: There is too much mind and not enough heart in their makeup to be effective with cats. However, their playful outlook and fresh and lively points of view may help them to understand their cats. The Gemini owner must cultivate patience and affection and try to create a restful atmosphere in the home rather than a stimulating, cluttered one. The Gemini owner's whole reaction to life lacks warmth and affection, but this is particularly important in the relationship with cats. There are many problems that pure reason alone will not solve, and one of them is controlling your cat.

Cancer

The Cancer owner has been described as the epitome of the caring owner. It is true that these people love cats and make the greatest amount of fuss over them, but they are not always wise in rearing them. The male Cancer owner is exacting, fussy, and critical of the cat, and keeps talking to the cat in negative tones until the cat becomes nervous. The Cancer mother dotes on her cat until it does something she does not like, then she rebukes it too sternly. She herself is full of tempers and has very little control over her own emotions; consequently, she is too harsh on her cat's behavior. She is both too easy and too hard—the cat never knows what is going on or going to happen. These owners give plenty of love, but their attitude is not sufficiently reasonable for bringing up young kittens, and although they are devoted owners, the atmosphere is too hysterical for the cat.

Leo

Leo owners of both sexes make, on general principles, rather good cat owners. The Leo female is particularly successful, though a little too dictatorial and dominant. For example, rather than letting a cat sleep where it likes, the female owner will quite often push the cat off

the seat, although her love is so sincere that the cat soon realizes its strength. Perhaps the greatest fault of owners of both sexes in the Leo sign is the desire to rule absolutely over the home and know where the cat is the whole time. Either the ruler demands too much attention from the cat or smothers the cat with attention, making the cats too dependent on the advantages that they receive in the home life. There is no doubt about the generosity and quality of the Leo's love for his or her cat, for it ranks first in the emotional response to cats of all the twelve signs of the Zodiac.

VIRGO

Virgos make excellent owners so far as the visual and material factors in life are concerned. The Virgo female notices everything the cat does and will often talk to friends about her cat. She is meticulous about her cat's appearance and grooming and instills in the cat very early in life a sense of method and order, so the cat will get set into a daily routine. The male Virgo owner has much the same attitudes as the Virgo female, and the most serious fault of both sexes is too much concern and being overprotective.

LIBRA

Libra owners are one of the best of the zodiac, with both sexes seeming to have an instinctive understanding of cats. They radiate a gentle camaraderie, which makes cats feel they are safe to be themselves. The Libra owner makes a cat enjoy learning the owner's rules, such as not jumping on the dining table. Owners show their love and devotion by an intelligent

direction of development, which is neither tyrannical nor too indulgent. In owners, the Libran qualities of judgment and balance are used to the greatest advantage.

SCORPIO

The Scorpio owner is, alas, one of the most prolific types and the poorest equipped to own cats. However, if Scorpio owners are open to understanding their faults, they can offer the cat a very good home. Owners of both sexes are impatient, ambitious, tyrannical, and clever. Their devotion to their cats is boundless, but their behavior lacks common sense and control. They are often harsh on their cat's behavior, and their methods of discipline are too severe. Scorpio owners must learn to harness their passions and look after their cats' needs, giving them the benefit of their own natural caring and loving gifts.

SAGITTARIUS

The female Sagittarian owner makes a better owner than the male, who is not sufficiently detailed in the caring of his cat and appears to be disinterested.

It has been said that these people have such a great interest in the world at large that it would not be asking too much of them to devote more attention to their cats. Yet the Sagittarian has a lot of love and affection to give to a loving cat. The female owner serves her cat with more specialized attention than the Sagittarian male. In fact, she has some of the Libran's good sense in the rearing of kittens and, in addition, often develops in them very early in life an interest in chasing a ball of string, chasing leaves, and having fun.

CAPRICORN

The female Capricorn owner is a far better owner than the Capricorn male. She is rather like the Virgo female owner in her dedicated supervision and concern for her cat and her persistent efforts to offer her cat the best living environment. Like the Virgo female owner, however, she sometimes errs on the side of commission rather than omission. She will at times push her cat beyond its capabilities, perhaps forgetting that the cat is not human. The male owner is far too exacting and severe. He resembles the Scorpio owner in that he has no patience with the affections that a cat needs. He is harsh and unsympathetic towards the cat and thinks only in terms of discipline, quite often forgetting the cat's natural hunting instincts. The male owner is quite often on the go, so a cat who enjoys rest is not well-suited with this male owner. Dominated by the planet Saturn, this type of owner can expect little but fear from his cat—unless he tempers his severity, he will lose out in the affection and love the cat has to offer.

AQUARIUS

Aquarian owners of both sexes make ideal cat owners. Aquarius is the humane sign, and the qualities dominant in their character are ideal for bringing up a happy and healthy cat. They give their cats the freedom to be themselves and feel comfortable without feeling pressured to seek the needed attention. The cat will soon learn to be patient and not be pushy with the owner, because the Aquarian owner will not forget about the cat's needs such as warmth, food, love, and attention. Aquarians always try to create a healthy environment for their cats, believing that this will engender long-lasting love in return.

PISCES

Pisces is a very fertile sign. Pisceans of both sexes make loving and devoted owners, although they are apt to be too indulgent. The highly developed Pisceans live such a remote existence that the practical but delicate problem of cat training eludes them. For the most part, this is too hard a job for Pisceans to work at seriously and consistently, leaving the cat not quite sure where it stands. Pisces owners enjoy the companionship of their cat. Supervision is something they try to avoid simply by letting the cat have its own way. Owners of this group might try to discipline themselves to the point where less agreeable cat development programs are faithfully undertaken.

FURTHER READING

Bryant, Mark. *The Complete Lexicat: A Cat Name Compendium*. Jersey City, NJ: Parkwest Publications Inc., 1995.

Buckle, Jane. *How to Massage Your Cat*. New York: Howell Book House, Macmillan, 1996.

Cooper, Paulette and Paul Noble. *277 Things Your Cat Wants You to Know*. Berkeley, CA: Ten Speed Press, 1997.

Fogle, Bruce. *First Aid for Cats: What to Do When Emergencies Happen*. New York: Penguin, 1997.

Ivory, Leslie Anne. *Star Cats: A Feline Zodiac*. Boston, MA: Bulfinch Press, 1998.

Jankowski, Connie. *Adopting Cats and Kittens*. New York: Howell Book House, Macmillan, 1993.

Loxton, Howard. *Cats (Spotter's Guide Series)*. Tulsa, OK: EDC Publishing, 1995.

Neville, Peter. *Do Cats Need Shrinks?: Cat Behavior Explained*. Chicago, IL: Contemporary Books, 1990.

Nilsen, Diana. *Your Pet's Horoscope*. St. Paul, MN: Llewellyn Publications, 1998.

Reyes, Simone; Ken Compton; and Patrick Caton (editor). *Astrology for Cats*. Glendale Heights, IL: Great Quotations, 1998.

Sameck, Stephanie. *A Cat's Guide to the Millennium: Spiritual Paths for the Enlightened Cat*. New York: Plume, Penguin Putnam Inc., 1997.

Webster, Richard. *Revealing Hands: How to Read Palms*. St. Paul, MN: Llewellyn Publications, 1994.

SPEED PAWMISTRY

OVERALL PAW SHAPE
(fussiness)

BEST SHAPE—big pads, slightly pointed at top, large pad and uppers equal length
SHORT—quick to hunt and train, no interest in picking over small bones, much energy
LONG and THIN—temperamental, likes examining details, strong imagination, romantic, susceptible
THICK—selfish
LARGE PAD LONGER THAN UPPER PAD AREA—indelicate, easily satisfied
UPPER PAD AREA LONGER THAN LARGE PAD—active mind, critical, good memory

NATURALLY RESTING PAW
(independence)

Which upper pads naturally fall apart?
1ST AND 2ND—independent thinker
3RD AND 4TH—independent actions
ALL WIDE APART—originality, self-reliance
ALL CURL UPWARDS—conventional, conforming, unimaginative
PADS TWITCHING—loves good things to eat and drink (too much = greed)

FEEL OF THE PAW
(confidence)

Best feel is moderately hard.
MOIST, DRY, HOT, or SPOTTY—nervous, shy, won't take initiative
COLD—poor circulation, inactive animal, no passion, recovering from recent illness
HARD—energy and perseverance
POINTED—activity with elegance
EXCESSIVELY HARD—lack of intelligence
SOFT—laziness of mind and body
SOFT and SQUARE—active body, lazy mind, lacking in loyalty
SOFT and SPATULATE—active mind, lazy body, training lessons may not be remembered

Skin
(irritability)

BEST SKIN—comfortable feel, clear and smooth
SOFT—impressionable
HARD—quarrelsome, fight-happy
MANY SMALL LINES—agitated life or ill health
WHITISH OR PALE PAW—selfishness

The Speed Pawmistry flash cards give you a simple and portable extra tool. Cut them out and glue them onto cardboard. Carry them around ready to be used when faced with a new cat.

Claws
(temper)

LARGE, CURVED AT BASE—good fortune
SHORT—criticising, contradicting
WIDER THAN LONG—obstinate
SQUARE AT BOTTOM—passionate, angry; steer clear
PINK OUTER EDGES—irritated
THIN, RIDGED, or HARD CLAWS—delicate health

Lines
(mental, physical, and emotional well-being)

LONG, NARROW, DEEP—healthy
CHAINED—health worries
Head Line
LONG, NARROW, EVEN—good mental balance; confident, impulsive
STRAIGHT—common sense, economy, care
SLOPING—good imagination but lacking in good judgment
GOES ONLY HALFWAY UP—selfish
CHAINED—too much variety, confused
Heart Line
NARROW, DEEP, STRAIGHT—emotional balance
LONG—noble, loving nature
SHORT—coldhearted, disloyal
BROKEN—many owners
BRANCHES—influenced by others
CHAINED—contemptuous

ASTROLOGICAL CHART FOR YOUR CAT

The signs of the zodiac are divided into fire, water, earth, and air signs and partake of the qualities of those elements. Each of the twelve signs rules a different part of the cat body, making this organ strong or sensitive according to the birth aspects.

ARIES—sign of leadership; governs head and face

TAURUS—sign of possessions and comfort, love and beauty; rules the neck and throat

GEMINI—sign of dual personality, short journeys, speed; governs shoulders and paws

CANCER—sign of home and mother; governs the stomach

LEO—sign of love and good breeding; governs the heart

VIRGO—sign of health and loyalty; governs the intestines

LIBRA—sign of partnership and cravings; governs the kidneys

SCORPIO—sign of inheritances and conditions surrounding the digestive functions; governs the organs of generation

SAGITTARIUS—sign of an adventurous cat, loves to run and play; governs the back

CAPRICORN—sign of success and authority; governs the knees

AQUARIUS—sign of friendship; governs the legs

PISCES—sign of isolation and contentment; governs the paws

The following table shows the four elements and the signs that are related to those elements.

FIRE—sign of leadership, fearlessness, adventure, playfulness: Aries, Leo, Sagittarius

WATER—sign of independence, homeliness, motherliness, strong will: Pisces, Cancer, Scorpio

EARTH—sign of love, beauty, health, and loyalty: Taurus, Virgo and Capricorn

AIR—sign of short journeys, speed, love of outdoors, love of human companionship: Gemini, Libra, Aquarius

THE CAT'S PAW

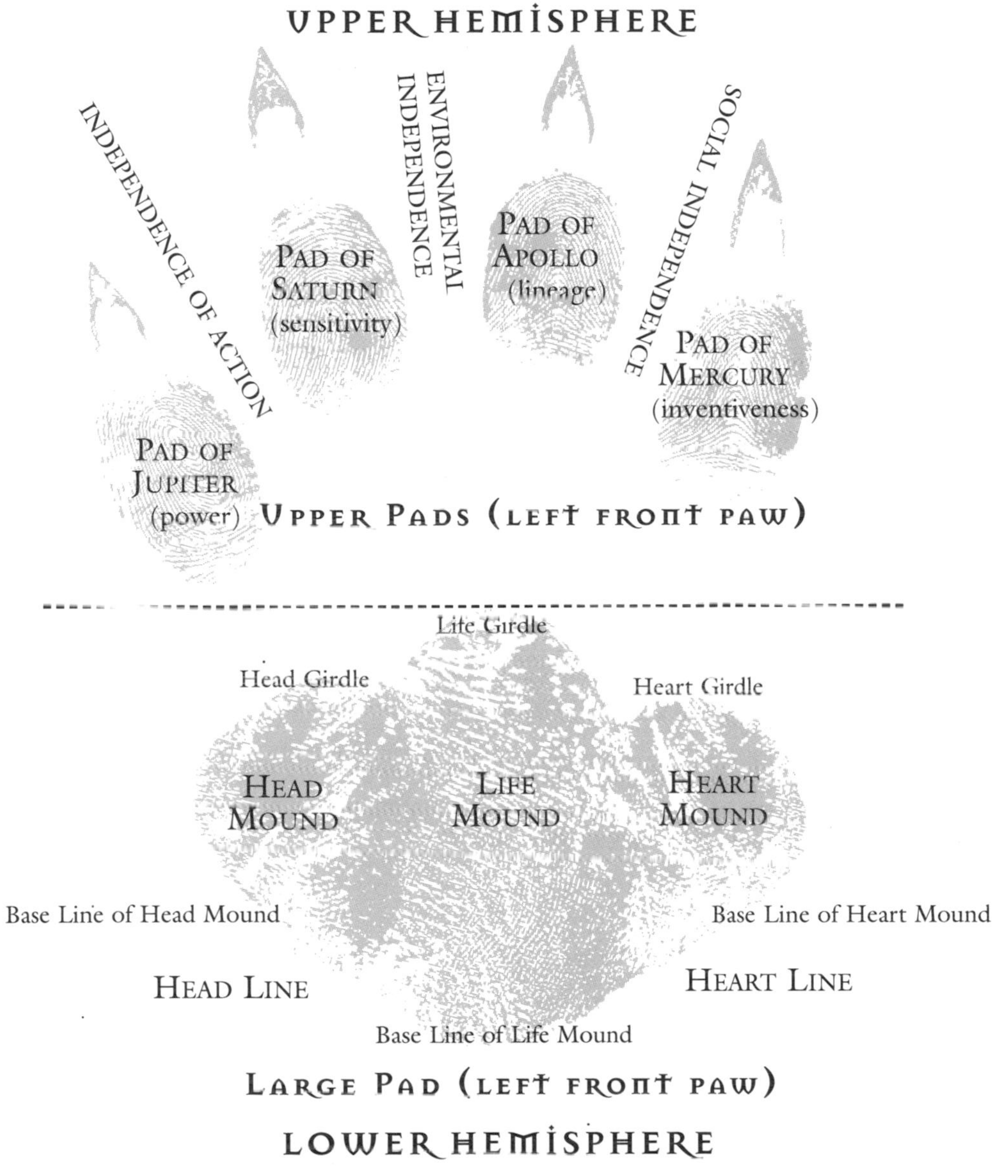

UPPER HEMISPHERE

INDEPENDENCE OF ACTION

ENVIRONMENTAL INDEPENDENCE

SOCIAL INDEPENDENCE

PAD OF
SATURN
(sensitivity)

PAD OF
APOLLO
(lineage)

PAD OF
MERCURY
(inventiveness)

PAD OF
JUPITER
(power)

UPPER PADS (LEFT FRONT PAW)

Life Girdle

Head Girdle

Heart Girdle

HEAD
MOUND

LIFE
MOUND

HEART
MOUND

Base Line of Head Mound

Base Line of Heart Mound

HEAD LINE

HEART LINE

Base Line of Life Mound

LARGE PAD (LEFT FRONT PAW)

LOWER HEMISPHERE

NOTES (CAT SCRATCHES)

 INDEX

MORE GREAT BOOKS FOR CATS AND THEIR OWNERS FROM TEN SPEED PRESS

WHY CATS PAINT
A Theory of Feline Aesthetics

by Heather Busch and Burton Silver

An unprecedented photographic record of cat creativity. "Nails the pretentiousness of art criticism to the wall"
—*Newsweek*

9 1/2 x 11 inches / 96 pages, full color
$16.95 paper, ISBN 0-89815-612-0
$18.95 cloth, ISBN 0-89815-623-8

COMPOSITION WITH CAT
Lost Masterpieces of the Twentieth Century

by William Warmack

This cat-alog of gorgeous feline artworks in the style of twentieth-century masters is a sly send-up of art, artists, cat lovers, and critics alike.

9 1/2 x 11 inches / 96 pages, full color
$16.95 paper, ISBN 0-89815-826-5
$24.95 cloth, ISBN 0-89815-923-7

277 SECRETS YOUR CAT WANTS YOU TO KNOW

by Paulette Cooper and Paul Noble

A purr fectly bewitching catalog of unusual and useful information, such as the 3 easiest tricks to teach your cat, the 25 things you didn't know about cat food, and the secret to picking out the best darn cat in the world.

5 1/2 x 8 1/2 inches / 256 pages
$8.95 paper, ISBN 0 89815 952 0

CATFLEXING
The Cat Lover's Guide to Weight Training, Aerobics, and Stretching

by Stephanie Jackson

Cat lover and fitness enthusiast Stephanie Jackson presents a revolutionary—okay, fine, downright wacky program that shows you how to use your cat to shape, tone, and trim your body.

8 1/2 x 8 7/8 inches / 112 pages
$12.95 paper, ISBN 0-89815-940-7

TEST YOUR CAT'S CREATIVE INTELLIGENCE
by Burton Silver

Here's a handy home test to determine whether your little precious has the potential to be a world-class artiste.

5 7/8 x 8 1/2 inches / 48 pages
$12.95 spiralbound case, ISBN 0-89815-879-6

Available from your local bookstore, or by ordering direct from the publisher.

Ten Speed Press • Celestial Arts • Tricycle Press
Box 7123, Berkeley, California 94707
Order phone (800) 841-2665 • Fax (510) 559-1629 • order@tenspeed.com • www.tenspeed.com

To Felicity

A Kirsty Melville Book

Ten Speed Press
P.O. Box 7123
Berkeley, California 94707
www.tenspeed.com

Originally published in 1998 by Penguin Books New Zealand

Distributed in Canada by Ten Speed Press Canada

Design by Dexter Fry and Libby Oda
Cover design by Paul Kepple
Astrological drawings by Liam Gerrard

Library of Congress Cataloging-in-Publication Data

Ring, Ken.
Pawmistry: how to read your cat's paws: your cat's personality revealed / Ken Ring and Paul Romhany.
        p.   cm.
    Includes bibliographical references (p.   ) and index.
    ISBN 1-58008-111-8 paper
    1. Cats—Miscellanea. 2. Astrology and pets. 3. Palmistry—Miscellanea. I. Romhany, Paul. II. Title
BF 1728.3.R55 1999
133' .25999752--dc21   99-23384
                                                                        CIP

First printing, 1999
Printed in Canada

1 2 3 4 5 6 7 8 9 10 — 03 02 01 00 99